Mark,

We hope this book helps
you to start "a legacy" with
Grace that will be passed
on for generations!

LE*the*GACY

What every father wants to leave his child

LE *the* GACY

STEVEN J. LAWSON

Multnomah Publishers *Sisters, Oregon*

THE LEGACY
published by Multnomah Books
a division of Multnomah Publishers, Inc.

and in association with the literary agency of Yates & Greer, LLP

© 1998 by Steven J. Lawson
International Standard Book Number: 1-57673-329-7

Cover photograph © 1998 by Bill Cannon

Unless otherwise noted, Scripture quotations are from:
New American Standard Bible (NASB) © 1960, 1977 by the Lockman Foundation

Also cited:
The Holy Bible, New International Version (NIV) © 1973, 1984 by International Bible
Society, used by permission of Zondervan Publishing House

The Holy Bible, New King James Version (NKJV)
© 1984 by Thomas Nelson, Inc.

The Holy Bible, King James Version (KJV)

Printed in the United States of America

For information:
MULTNOMAH PUBLISHERS, INC.
POST OFFICE BOX 1720
SISTERS, OREGON 97759

Library of Congress Cataloging-in-Publication Data:
Lawson, Steven J.
    The legacy : What every father wants to leave his child/by Steven J. Lawson.
       p. cm. ISBN 1-57673–329–7 (alk. paper)
    1. Fathers—Religious life. 2. Parenting—Religious aspects—Christianity.
    I. Title.
BV4529.L28   1998   97–36396
248.8'421—dc21   CIP

98 99 00 01 02 03 04 05 — 10 9 8 7 6 5 4 3 2 1

This book is affectionately dedicated to
my precious daughter,
Grace Anne
Sweet Girl, you are a priceless jewel
and a constant delight to my heart.

May God grant you the grace
to one day pass on
"the legacy"
to your children.

"Many daughters have done nobly,
but you excel them all.
Charm is deceitful and beauty is vain,
but a woman who fears the Lord,
she shall be praised."
PROVERBS 31:29–30

ACKNOWLEDGMENTS

I want to thank the team at Multnomah for their support in this project, especially Don Jacobson, Matt Jacobson, and Bob Krupp.

I want to express my deepest appreciation to some special people who have helped me in this book—Chuck Gschwend, Jane and Dan Dumas, and Paul Lamey.

Likewise, I want to thank the Wednesday Morning Men's Discipleship Group at Dauphin Way Baptist Church with whom I shared this material and who served as a catalyst for this book.

Finally, I must thank my wife, Anne, who provided me with great encouragement throughout this project. Also, a special thanks to my four children, Andrew, James, Grace Anne, and John who, along with Anne, faithfully prayed for this book, lived it with me, and graciously allowed me to share several incidents involving themselves.

CONTENTS

PART THREE: BEQUEATHING A LEGACY

INTRODUCTION

This is a book about fathering. I write not as a spectator sitting idly in the stands, but as a dad down on the field, fully involved with four young children of my own. My wife Anne and I have three sons—Andrew, James, and John—and a daughter Grace Anne. I eat, sleep, and drink fathering.

Not a day goes by that I do not face some new adventure in being a dad. In addition, I pastor a growing church with lots of dads. My point is, I'm into fathering.

If you're like me, you want to be the best dad you can be. But the challenge is *how. How* can I excel as a father? In this book, I want to show you in practical ways how to be the dad God *wants* you to be.

Let me tell you right up front, everything I have to say will come straight out of the Bible. I believe the Scriptures are the inspired Word of God. And, as such, they are eternal and timeless, and just as relevant today as when they were first written. Although centuries old, the Bible is more up to date than tomorrow's newspaper. Through the pages of His Word, God is still speaking today to every dad. Quite frankly, we simply need to discover what God has to say and then put it into daily practice.

We've heard from the gurus, the experts, and the professionals. Now, don't we need to hear afresh from God? I will share from my own experience as a father, but only to illustrate God's truth, not replace it.

The theme of this book revolves around leaving a legacy—a *spiritual* legacy—*the legacy* that you leave for your children. By that I mean the lasting influence every dad passes down to his children. We are all leaving a set of core values for our kids that will impact their lives for years to come. But we must be careful that we bequeath the *right* core values—*God's* core values. Every dad needs to leave behind solid values like godliness and love, virtues like respect and discipline, qualities like obedience and hard work.

Admittedly, these are becoming outdated and, yes, they are vanishing from our present-day scene. But I believe we can recapture them and impart them to our children. Only then will they possess a spiritual legacy for years to come, long after we are gone.

In addition, we will talk about the spiritual warfare our kids are facing. How can we equip them right now with a bullet-proof faith? How can we send them out into a hostile world to stand victoriously? How can we pray for them to remain safe and in the protective hands of God? We'll discuss these things and map out a prayer strategy.

Now I know, as you pick up this book, you may be thinking that you've already blown it as a father. Maybe you're wondering if it's too late to get back into the game with your kids. Maybe you've been an "absentee dad" for years. Maybe you've brought the wrong influences upon your home. You're asking yourself, "Is it too late?"

Be assured, *failure is never final as long as there is the grace of God.* Nothing is impossible with God. He transcends time and, by His grace, can make up for our lost years. When God chooses to act, He can do more in six months that we in our own efforts can do in six decades. But we must get serious with Him *now!*

Dads, join me in the journey of this book. We have the most exciting, yet challenging job in the world. It's been said, the job of fathering is the one job you begin with no experience, and once you figure it out, you're out of a job. I don't believe it has to be that way. I believe that God's Word can equip us *today* to be successful dads with our kids while they are still at home and under our direct influence.

So use this book to help prepare you for the greatest job you will ever have—the job of being a *dad!*

Steven J. Lawson
Mobile, Alabama

PART 1

BIRTHING
A LEGACY

CHAPTER 1

THE GREATEST INHERITANCE ANY FATHER CAN LEAVE HIS CHILD

The Legacy of a Dad's Life

TELL ME WHO YOUR FATHER IS AND I'LL TELL YOU WHO YOU ARE.

—*Anonymous*

Every father leaves a legacy with his children—no exceptions. The only question is, *what kind* of legacy?

A few years ago, a team of New York state sociologists attempted to calculate the influence of a father's life on his children and the following generations. In this study, they researched two men who lived at the same time in the 18th century. One was Max Jukes, the other Jonathan Edwards. The legacy that each of these men left their descendants stands as a study in contrasts; they are as different as night and day.

Max Jukes was an unbeliever, a man of no principles. His wife also lived and died in unbelief. What kind of lasting influence did he leave his family? Among the 1,200 known descendants of Max Jukes were:

♦ 440 lives of outright debauchery
♦ 310 paupers and vagrants
♦ 190 public prostitutes
♦ 130 convicted criminals
♦ 100 alcoholics
♦ 60 habitual thieves

♦ 55 victims of impurity
♦ 7 murderers

Research shows that not a one of Jukes' descendants made a significant contribution to society—not one! To the contrary, this notorious family collectively cost the state of New York $1,200,000.

Not much of a legacy.

What about the family of Jonathan Edwards? Regarded as the most brilliant mind America ever produced, Edwards was a noted pastor and astute theologian. This renowned scholar was the instrument of God used to bring about the Great Awakening in colonial America. Later, he served as the president of Princeton College.

Jonathan Edwards came from a godly heritage and married Sarah, a woman of great faith. Together, they sought to leave an entirely different kind of legacy. Among his male descendants were:

♦ 300 clergymen, missionaries, or theological professors
♦ 120 college professors
♦ 110 lawyers
♦ over 60 physicians
♦ over 60 authors of good books
♦ 30 judges
♦ 14 presidents of universities
♦ numerous giants in American industry
♦ 3 U.S. congressmen
♦ 1 vice-president of the United States

There is scarcely any great American industry that has not had one of Jonathan Edwards descendants as its chief promoter.[1] Such is the lasting influence of one godly man.

Now, *that's* a legacy!

Every man leaves a lasting influence on his children that will affect future generations for centuries to come. But let's face it, not all legacies are the same. Some are productive, others are destructive. Some are illustrious, others are infamous. How you live your life will affect generations to come. The only question is, what kind of a legacy will you leave behind?

THIS IS YOUR LIFE

To help you answer that question, I want you to imagine that you have just walked into a church to attend a funeral service. The mood is somber, the crowd quiet. Loved ones are making their way past the open casket for the final viewing of the body. Many are weeping. Some are wiping their eyes with handkerchiefs. A few stand gazing at the lifeless body.

The specified time has now come for the service to begin. As the minister approaches the pulpit, he motions for the congregation to rise. The family of the deceased slowly proceeds down the center aisle to the front.

Anxiously, you look up to identify the family. As you peer into the face of each family member, you are in for the shock of your life. Suddenly, you realize this is *your family!*

You are attending... *your funeral!*

In stunned disbelief, you respond to the minister's directions for the congregation to be seated. He begins by expressing his feelings of appreciation for your life. What he says is nice and flattering. But at the same time, his words are generic and impersonal.

Let's be honest, it's the words of your family, those *closest* to you that matter most. What will *your wife* say about you? What will *your children* say?

The minister finishes his eulogy and motions to your children to come to the pulpit. They approach the platform, waiting their turn to speak about how you have influenced their lives. One by one, your kids reflect on their years with you and share their remembrances of you as their dad. They recall incidents you have long since forgotten. They remember your impact, reflect on your character, and recite your virtues.

At this point, all you can do is listen. With riveted attention, you hang on their every word. These are the most important sentences you will ever hear anyone speak about you. Your lasting success as a dad is measured by what they say.

All imagination aside, *if you died today, what would your children remember you for? What would be your legacy to them?*

What your children take from your life, in large measure, will define your legacy as a dad. Your lasting influence upon their lives will mark whether or not you lived successfully as a dad. *This* will be your legacy.

WHAT IS A LEGACY?

What comes to your mind when you hear the word *legacy?*

Most often, we think of a financial inheritance that is passed down from one generation to the next. A legacy conjures up images of hard assets, international real estate, multiple bank accounts, and blue chip stocks. And rightly so. The Bible itself teaches that leaving a monetary legacy for one's children is honorable and commendable. The book of Proverbs notes that a godly father desires to leave an inheritance for his children that will secure their future and improve their standard of living. Solomon writes:

A good man leaves an inheritance to his children's children. (Proverbs 13:22)

Further, the sage states:

House and wealth are an inheritance from fathers. (Proverbs 19:14)

But as desirable as it is for a father to leave a financial legacy, there are limitations, even dangers, in leaving behind the worldly possessions of this world for his children. Many a young person has been ruined by the sudden acquisition of wealth because they did not possess the maturity, nor the character, to handle it. In addition, a financial legacy doesn't last. Neither can it bring happiness—not *true* happiness. Jesus said life does not consist in the possessions we own, nor in the things we have.

Instead, I want to point you toward a different kind of legacy. One that money cannot buy and taxes cannot take away. One which is intangible, invisible, and eternal. One far more valuable than silver or gold. I'm talking about a *spiritual* legacy, one that will truly enrich our children's lives, mold their character, and impact their eternal destiny. A *godly* legacy is the only legacy *really* worth leaving.

At this point you may be asking, "What exactly is a *spiritual* legacy?"

A spiritual legacy is passing down to the next generation what matters most. Your faith in Jesus Christ and the core values of His eternal kingdom. It is the deliberate transferring of spiritual riches from your life to your kids. It is a portfolio of godly virtues being invested into their lives. Simply put, it is your *godly* influence imparted to your children for generations to come.

Let's face it, far more important than leaving a financial estate is the bequeathing of a spiritual inheritance. Long after whatever personal investments you may leave your children are spent, a spiritual legacy will only compound daily and pay rich dividends throughout all eternity. The man who leaves *only* a financial inheritance for his children leaves them poor. But the man who leaves a spiritual legacy for his family, whatever size his financial inheritance may be, leaves them rich.

The Bible says, "A righteous man walks in his integrity; his children are blessed after him" (Proverbs 20:7, NKJV). In other words, a man's personal integrity and righteous life becomes the greatest blessing for those who follow after him.

FOR DADS ONLY

To bring this spiritual legacy into focus, I want to draw our attention in this book to one key verse—Ephesians 6:4—as well as survey its surrounding context. Ephesians 6:4 is the only verse in the New Testament—along with its companion verse, Colossians 3:21—that is addressed *exclusively* to dads. This verse calls for every father's careful attention and demands our serious response. Here's what God says:

> And fathers, do not provoke your children to anger, but bring them
> up in the discipline and instruction of the Lord. (Ephesians 6:4)

Notice, God specifically addresses this instruction to *fathers,* not *mothers.* Nor is it addressed to *fathers and mothers.* But to fathers exclusively. Why do you think He does this? Because biblical manhood calls us, as men, to be the spiritual leaders of our homes. We did not volunteer for the position, nor were we elected. Instead, we were appointed by the Lord Himself to be the point men of our families.

As a result, it is every father's responsibility as the head of his home to prepare, pass down, and preserve a spiritual inheritance for his children. We have been chosen by God to leave certain essential core values—*godly virtues,* if you will—for the next generation.

I challenge you to think through two questions. What are your core values? What are you willing to die for?

Identifying your core values will reveal what *really* makes you tick. It will help you understand why you make certain decisions, why you are excited about certain things, why certain circumstances arouse you. Writing down what is most important in your life will help clarify your own personal values. Whatever they are, this is the lasting legacy that must be carefully deposited into your children's lives.

Unquestionably, the heartbeat of every Christian father must be his personal faith in Jesus Christ, and out of that flows the non-negotiables of the kingdom of God. This is what *must* be passed on to our children.

CORE VALUES—WHAT ARE THEY?

Core values are those non-negotiable, essential principles and timeless truths that permeate the totality of our being. Core values are what count. They are the hills worth dying on. They are the heartbeat of any individual or group. Core values are those common principles which unite any group together. And our families are no different.

Your family, like mine, is defined, directed, and driven by the core values that have been embraced and put into practice in your home. Today, if I was to ask your wife and children what your family's common values are, how would they respond? Can they put their finger on your pulse?

Wise is the father who defines his family's core values carefully and instills them in his children successfully. Whether we recognize it or not, every family has them. But not every family has the *right* core values, those articulated in the Word of God. So, we must look to the Scriptures if we are to pass on the *correct* core values to our children.

In this book, I will take Ephesians 6:4, along with it's surrounding context, and identify the core values that every father must build into his children. As Paul addressed the fathers of his day, so he speaks to us today. The following is an overview of these bedrock values upon which Scripture places a premium:

- ◆ A Legacy of *Godliness* (Ephesians 5:18–21)
- ◆ A Legacy of *Love* (Ephesians 5:22–33)
- ◆ A Legacy of *Obedience* (Ephesians 6:1)
- ◆ A Legacy of *Respect* (Ephesians 6:2–3)
- ◆ A Legacy of *Gentleness* (Ephesians 6:4a)

♦ A Legacy of *Maturity* (Ephesians 6:4b)
♦ A Legacy of *Discipline* (Ephesians 6:4c)
♦ A Legacy of *Wisdom* (Ephesians 6:4d)
♦ A Legacy of *Responsibility* (Ephesians 6:5–9)
♦ A Legacy of *Strength* (Ephesians 6:10–17)

Gentlemen, here is the only legacy worth leaving. Whether we ever become anyone important in this world is irrelevant. Whether we leave anything of great monetary value to our children is secondary. But whether we leave a spiritual inheritance to our sons and daughters is *everything!*

In the course of this book, I want to walk you through each of these core values, define them from God's Word, and show you how to build them into the lives of your children. And in the process, we will be better equipped to carry out our God-given responsibilities as a father. So join me now in what could revolutionize your family for generations to come.

HEIR TO A DREAM

Consider the legacy Press Maravich left for his son Pete. As the head basketball coach at Clemson, Press chose to pour his life into his young son, developing him into one of the premier athletes of our time. Pistol Pete played college basketball for his father at Louisiana State University, becoming the most prolific scorer in college basketball history. Under his dad's coaching, he became a three-time All-American and was the College Basketball Player of the Year. Upon graduation, Pete showcased his talents in the NBA, excelling at the highest level of the game.

But the acquiring of extraordinary basketball skills was not the greatest legacy Pete received from his father. More importantly, he received his father's character, work ethic, and discipline—all virtues that pointed his young life in the right direction.

Years later as Pete Maravich was ready to be inducted into the Basketball Hall of Fame in Springfield, Massachusetts, he wrote in his autobiography *Heir to a Dream* that this highest of all honors was, in reality, the fulfillment of his father's dream for his life. During his college days at LSU, Pete told his dad that if he ever made it to the Basketball Hall of Fame, he would refuse the award and say it was being given to the wrong person.

"Give the award to my Dad," Pete always told his father he would say, "because there is no way in the world I deserve the honor before he does."

As Pete Maravich sat on the platform beside the other inductees into the Hall of Fame—including legendary NBA greats like Rick Barry, Walt Frazier and other stars—he could only reflect upon memories of his dad's countless hours of devotion.

At that moment, Press Maravich lay bedridden with cancer, unable to attend the very induction ceremony for which he had trained Pete for so many years. In a matter of a few weeks, Press would be dead. When Pete's name "Peter Maravich," was announced—appropriately, it was also his father's name—he recalled his father's commitment to help him become the best he could be. Later, Pistol Pete reflected upon that moment:

> As I look back now, I finally feel as though I understand my *inheritance*. Dad handed me something beautiful and precious, and I will always be indebted to him. He gave me his life full of instruction and encouragement. He gave me hope in hopeless situations and laughter in the face of grim circumstances. Dad gave me an example of discipline unequaled, dedication unmatched. He gave me the privilege of seeing an unwavering faith when the darkness of life and death surrounded him.
>
> But, more than anything, my father became a symbol of what love and compassion can do in anyone's life, and I am happy to accept that love as his heir to a dream.[2]

Men, that's what it means to leave a legacy with our children long after we're gone. The lasting influence of a father's life on those whom you love most will pay dividends long into eternity. Press Maravich passed on the legacy of his life, and so can you and I.

The greatest legacy you and I will ever leave our family is our faith in God. Long after we're gone, a godly inheritance will enrich their lives profoundly.

Some men build careers. Others erect empires. But the rarest of men leave legacies.

What are *you* leaving?

CHAPTER 2

THEY'LL BE GONE BEFORE YOU KNOW IT

The Legacy You Must Leave Now

NOBODY ON HIS DEATHBED EVER SAID: I WISH
I'D SPENT MORE TIME AT THE OFFICE.
—*Peter Lynch*

Every father experiences unforgettable moments that are indelibly etched upon his mind. November 22, 1982 was one such moment for me.

My wife, Anne, was four months pregnant when I took her to the doctor for a routine checkup. As the nurse led us back into a waiting room, she jokingly said to Anne, "You look a little bit larger than normal. I wonder if you are going to have twins."

We were staring at one another dumbfounded when the doctor walked in and made the same assessment, saying, "I think we need an ultrasound because it looks like something unusual is going on here. You may be having twins."

"Wow, twins!" I shouted, pumping my fists into the air. "Wouldn't that be exciting!" All the while, Anne was trying to recover from the initial shock.

So the nurse led us down the hall for the ultrasound. As Anne lay down on the table, the nurse turned out the lights and began to rub the machine over her stomach. All three of us stared eagerly at the overhead screen, waiting to see what would be projected onto the wall. Before our watching eyes, the head and the pulsating heartbeat of a living person could be clearly seen. By this point, Anne was squeezing my hand so hard I was losing circulation.

Then the nurse uttered those now immortal words, "Oh, my goodness!" she exclaimed. "There are *two* in there!"

I got so lightheaded, I felt faint. The nurse caught me, lowered me into a chair, and laid a cold washcloth across my forehead—leaving Anne completely unattended on the table, draped in only a sheet.

Regaining my composure, I stared back up at the overhead screen where I had been watching our family grow by the minute, and told the nurse, "Keep looking, see if there's *anyone else* in there."

Special Delivery

With the subsequent births of our other two children—and, yes, those came only one at a time—the excitement and adventure of being a father has only escalated. I think the full magnitude of being a father hit me the hardest, though, when our daughter Grace Anne was born. That was because hers was the only birth for which I was actually present in the delivery room.

I had my own stool to sit on at the head of the operating table. I even had my own nurse to catch me if I passed out. Fortunately, a curtain was raised over Anne's midsection so that I couldn't see all of the action that was taking place down there.

When the dramatic moment came for Grace Anne to enter the world, the doctor delivered her and held her up from behind the curtain for me to see. "Look, Steve!" he exclaimed. "Look what God has given you!"

Immediately, we bonded as father and child. With a rush of excitement, I looked at Grace Anne and shouted enthusiastically, "It's a *boy!* It's a *boy!*"

Unfortunately, I had mistaken the umbilical cord for, errr…something else. *What a boy, huh?*

In a state of disbelief, the doctor stared at me and said, "Where did you go to school, son?"

I said, "Texas Tech," somewhat embarrassed for my alma mater.

At that moment, I once again felt the enormous responsibility of fatherhood placed squarely upon my trembling shoulders. Not something to be taken lightly, I was reentering the role of fatherhood again with fear and trepidation, this time the father of a precious baby girl.

Since that time, I have been impressed with how little time I really have with my kids before they leave our home. With each passing day, I am made more aware that our time together as a family is but a passing vapor.

THE CLOCK IS TICKING

This really struck home with me when I was talking with the pulpit committee of the church which I now pastor. As I was visiting in their home and wrestling with the decision, an even more important issue emerged. The conversation turned to one of the couple's two grown sons who had recently moved away from home. The wife then made a statement that hit me like a ton of bricks.

As she considered how the years had so quickly passed with their own children, she reflected and said, "Steve, enjoy your children while you've got them. The time will pass faster than you realize." Then she made the statement that still reverberates in my soul.

"Steve, they'll be gone before you know it."

Those words sank deeply into my heart. Immediately, I added up how many years I had remaining with each of my children at home and was struck with how little time there was. A lump the size of a basketball swelled up in my throat. Instantly, my eyes teared up and my voice began to crack.

At first, the thought of starting a new work with all its competing time demands made me want to withdraw to a secluded area and be alone with my family. And yet, I knew that the call of God upon my life would not allow me to run and hide.

Throughout the rest of the evening, I kept hearing those sobering words echoing over and over in my mind, as if they were being interjected into every conversation, *"They'll be gone before you know it.... They'll be gone before you know it...."*

Before I go any further, let me ask you, "How many years do *you* have left with your children?" Seriously, stop right now. Go ahead, add it up. How many more years do you have with your children at home? It doesn't take a rocket scientist to grasp the brevity of life regarding the time we have left with our family. Has that reality gripped you yet?

Men, no matter how many years you have left with your children, you must act *now* if you're going to maximize what little time remains. We would all do well to pay attention to the words of the apostle Paul that speak directly to this issue. May his inspired words sink deeply into our hearts:

Therefore be careful how you walk, not as unwise men, but as wise, making the most of your time, because the days are evil. So then do not be foolish but understand what the will of the Lord is. (Ephesians 5:15–17)

These verses challenge us to invest our time wisely. Today, if anyone needs to maximize their time, it's we dads with our children! Simply stated, these verses present a fourfold challenge for every father. We need to *wise up, buy up, look up,* and *grow up!* Let's look at each of these carefully now.

CHALLENGE #1:
DADS, WISE UP!
*Therefore be careful how you walk,
not as unwise men, but as wise.*
EPHESIANS 5:15

Let's face it, there is not a father with enough personal insight, discernment, experience, and understanding to adequately guide his children through the complex maze of this chaotic, changing world. We must have God's wisdom if we are to lead our families effectively, or they will self-destruct in a heart-beat.

TWO PATHS, TWO DESTINIES

In this verse, the apostle contrasts "unwise" and "wise." In reality, these are the only two paths before every father—the *world's wisdom* versus *God's wisdom*. And the two are diametrically opposed to each other. What's so dangerous about them is, at first glance, they often look and sound very similar. But, in reality, they are as different as heaven and hell. And that's exactly where they lead.

Recently, I was in an airport walking down the corridor, and saw two terminal gates closely positioned to each other. One read "Departing Flight: Los Angeles," and the other "Departing Flight: New York." They were so close together that they even shared the same waiting area. As I looked at those two gates, I thought how easy it would be to board the wrong plane. Although the two gates were adjacent, they led to opposite ends of our country.

That's the way it is with worldly and godly wisdom. At first glance, they may appear to be very close, but let me assure you, they will take you in two opposite directions. So, be careful which plane you board. Not only will it determine your destiny, but it will mark your children's future as well.

Worldly wisdom is man-centered, relative, pragmatic, and constantly changing. It is collected from a variety of sources—culture, tradition, humanistic philosophy, and personal experiences—and it leads to *destruction*. But God's wisdom comes down from above, meaning it doesn't originate with man, and is holy, righteous, and gentle (James 3:13)—and leads to *life and godliness*.

Unfortunately, most fathers never see where the path of worldly thinking will lead their family. Not until it is too late. The Bible says, "There is a way that seems right to a man, but its end is the way of death" (Proverbs 14:12). Although the road signs read "blessing," in reality, the way of worldly wisdom leads to "destruction." That's the irony of this deadly deception! Thinking that they are actually *helping* their children, such fathers are *harming* them.

No wonder the apostle Paul says, *"Be careful how you walk"* (Ephesians 5:15). We must take pains to lead our families down the right path. Why? Because it will determine *where* your children end up, *how* they end up, *with whom* they end up, and *what* they end up doing and being.

Dads, wise up and get on the right track—pursue *God's* wisdom!

WHAT IS WISDOM?

Let's get a better picture of what wisdom is. In the Old Testament, the Hebrew word for "wise" (*hoekma*) was used to describe a craftsman's ability to skillfully complete a particular task. For example, the workmen who built the tabernacle took pieces of wood and cloth material and carved the boards and weaved the tapestries into beautiful objects of art for all to admire.

In like manner, wisdom is the ability to take the Word of God and skillfully weave it into the fabric of one's life so that the end result is a beautiful tapestry, a life lived as God intended. Wisdom is the God-given ability to *see* life from God's perspective with penetrating insight, to *size up* situations with discernment for what they truly are, and then select the best solution to achieve the highest ends. See, size up, and select—*that's wisdom!*

In the New Testament, the Greek word for wisdom (*sophos*) retains the same idea of skillful living. James 3:13 says, "Who among you is wise and understanding? Let him show by his good behavior his deeds in the gentleness of wisdom." In other words, the wise man is the one who is proficient in the daily living of practical godliness. He knows God's Word and is able to apply it to every area of his life, including his fathering as it relates to his children. Wisdom, then, is applying God's Word to God's will for God's glory.

Men, we need wisdom to lead our families. We must be able to see into our kids' lives and understand the world in which they live with God-given insight. We must grasp how God has uniquely made them and discern what forces are impacting their lives. Then we must be able to take timeless truths from Scripture and skillfully weave them into the fabric of their lives so that they can be all that God intends them to be.

CHALLENGE #2:
DADS, BUY UP!
Making the most of your time.
EPHESIANS 5:16

The apostle goes on to say in the next verse that, as we walk in wisdom, we must do so with a sense of urgency—"making the most of your time."

We are busier than we've ever been before. Dad's are rising earlier, getting to the office sooner, working harder, cramming more into the day, staying later, and traveling more. More and more is being crammed into less and less. The information super highway with its mobile phones, faxes, and personal computers—which intended to give us more time—is causing family time to shrink like a cheap sweater.

Fathers once worked in the field together with their children in an agrarian society, or worked together side-by-side in the family store. The industrial revolution changed all that and fathers began to work outside the home. This dramatic transition literally jolted the role of men in America. This separation has only been compounded in this high-tech age of corporate America. Many fathers now sleep at home, but live at work.

WHERE HAS OUR TIME GONE?

Harvard economist Juliet Schor explains that the average American will work the equivalent of one month longer this year than twenty years ago. Not only that, but there are record rates of overtime and moonlighting.[2] Men are busier than ever before. Where has our time gone?

Since 1973, the amount of leisure time enjoyed by the average American has decreased 37 percent since 1973 from 26.2 hours to 16.6 hours. Over the same period, the average work week, including commuting, has jumped from under 41 hours to nearly 47 hours.

In a lifetime, the average American will spend:

- ♦ *six months* sitting at traffic lights waiting for them to change.
- ♦ *one year* searching through desk clutter looking for misplaced objects.
- ♦ *eight months* opening junk mail.
- ♦ *two years* unsuccessfully returning phone calls.
- ♦ *five years* waiting in lines.
- ♦ *three years* in meetings.[2]

In addition, the average person will:

- ♦ commute *45 minutes* every day.
- ♦ be interrupted *75 times* every day.
- ♦ receive *600 advertising messages* every day (television, newspapers, magazines, radio, billboards).
- ♦ travel *7,700 miles* every year.
- ♦ watch *1,700 hours* of television every year.
- ♦ open *600 pieces of mail* every year.[3]

As a result, expressions like *no time, lack of time, not enough time,* or *being out of time* fill our speech. Trying to get more time, we "borrow" time from one area of our life only to end up with even less time where it really counts. As a result, we must make the most of our time.

THE TIME IS NOW!

There are two key words from verse 16 that command our attention. The first is "time" (Greek word, *kairos*) which refers not to clock or calendar time (that's a different Greek word, *chronos*), but to a unique opportunity within time to do something significant. It signifies a moment in time—a one-time, passing opportunity—that is most strategic and pivotal. As this relates to fathering, the Bible is saying, "Take advantage of the time that you have with your children while you have it. You will never have this moment again."

A few years ago, a Kodak commercial featured a series of snapshots of a father with his daughter. As different pictures flash on the screen, string music plays in the background, while a singer croons, "These are the times of your life."

First, there is a picture of the dad holding his little girl at birth. *Click,* the picture instantly changes and he is feeding his baby in a highchair with baby food all over himself. *Click,* the picture changes again and the dad is helping his little girl learn to ride a bicycle down the neighborhood sidewalk. *Click,* now he is teaching his teenage daughter to drive a car. *Click,* now dad is asleep on the sofa, waiting up for her to come in from a date.

As the commercial builds, *click,* the father is wearing a tuxedo, standing at the altar with his daughter, now a beautiful young woman. He is staring misty-eyed at her while she is staring at her groom.

Listen, the message is clear. *They'll be gone before you know it!*

These snapshots of time with our children are quickly passing and are irretrievable and irreplaceable. The camera is clicking whether we're ready or not. And there are only so many snapshots left on the roll. We must make every opportunity count!

In order to make the most of our time, we must cut out many good things in our schedule to make room for the best things.

Film maker Walt Disney was ruthless in cutting out anything that was good if it competed with what was best. Ward Kimball, one of the animators for *Snow White,* recalls working 240 days on a 4 1/2 minute sequence in which the dwarfs made soup for Snow White and almost destroyed the kitchen in the process. Disney thought it was funny, but he decided the scene stopped the flow of the picture, so out it went. Only by sacrificing good things could the film be the best.[4]

That's how we must be! When the film of our lives is played by God on the final day, will it be as great as it might be? A lot will depend upon whether or not we eliminated good things in order to make way for the "great" things God wanted to do with our children.

Psalm 90:12 says, "So teach us to number our days that we may present to Thee a heart of wisdom." Wise is the father who maximizes his time and captures his opportunities with his children. We only have so much time, so we must make the most of it.

BUY UP THE TIME!

There is a second key Greek word in Ephesians 5:16 (*exagorazo*), translated "make the most of," which requires our attention. It means "to buy something out of the marketplace." In the King James Version, it is translated "redeem." The word was used in ancient times of buying a slave in the open market and by paying a purchase price. What Paul is getting at here is, we must buy up what opportunities we have with our children like a valuable commodity.

Few individuals have been able to capture human emotion and transfer it onto canvas like the artistic genius of Norman Rockwell. One of his paintings, *Breaking Home Ties,* always touches my heart deeply.

In this classic painting, a young teenage boy sits on the running board of the family pickup truck along with his father. The face of the young boy is beaming as he waits to catch the bus on the side of a country lane that will take him to college. His suitcase is packed, his textbooks are at his side, his future is ever before him.

But the countenance of the father is somber. For him, this departure means a sad farewell. The close of an era. He knows the time has come to say good-bye. A part of his home is now leaving, but more than that, a part of his heart.

If you are a father, you can surely relate to the heart tug of this scene. I think about it often as I tuck my children into bed. I think about it when I wrestle with them on the den floor. I think about it when I play basketball in the driveway with them. I think about it every summer when we pull out of our driveway for our family vacation. The day will come, sooner than I realize, when I will have to say good-bye to my children.

We must redeem these moments while we have them. No matter how mundane to us, they are very monumental to our children.

The following story illustrates the point.

At the constant request of his young son, a busy dad took a day off to go fishing. It was just the two of them. Leaving behind a desk cluttered with unfinished business, the father drove to a secluded lake where they spent the day together fishing, rowing, talking, and fishing some more.

Throughout the day, all the father could think about was the pressing deadlines that he had left behind. Phone calls to return. Projects to complete. Assignments to finish. Meetings to make.

Years later, their two diaries were discovered as each recorded what the day had meant to them. In the father's journal was recorded, "Took my son fishing. Another day lost." But in the boy's dairy, the entry read, "Spent the day with dad. It was one of the greatest days of my life."

Unlike money, time comes to all of us in equal amounts. In fact, everyone has the same amount—twenty-four hours a day. However, we are all confronted with a wide variety of choices in our use of that time. In the final analysis, how we use our time depends upon our priorities. We make the time for what we think is important.

The legacy will never be passed on to our children without the wise investment of our most precious commodity—time. Dads, buy up the time while you can.

They'll be gone before you know it.

CHALLENGE #3:
DADS, LOOK UP!
Because the days are evil.
EPHESIANS 5:16

The world in which our children live is greatly different from the one in which we grew up. If we are to lead our families effectively, we must have an astute awareness of the times in which we live. We must know the forces they face and the dangers that await them. Not surprisingly, Paul warns us that "the days are evil" (Ephesians 5:16). A wise father will discern the times and be prepared to steer his children through the uncharted, dangerous waters of today's society.

Dads, we must "look up" and see our world for what it is, not for what it once was, or what we would like it to be. We must take off our rose-colored glasses and see that our society is collapsing. We must also understand that the fall of every great nation was caused by the destruction of the traditional family unit. Nation's crumble from within, not from without.

History Repeats Itself

What caused the Roman family system to collapse in Paul's day are the same evil forces that are causing the American family to fall apart today. Divorce, relaxed moral standards, adultery, promiscuity, loss of respect for children and child rearing, and the decline in status of parenthood all accompanied the weakening of the Roman family. And these are destroying the American family today. Listen to these statistics:

♦ 60% of the children born in the nineties will live in a single parent home for part of their childhood.[5]

♦ One-fourth of the girls in the United States and one-tenth of the boys have been sexually abused.[6]

♦ Three out of five teens will try an illicit drug.[7]

♦ 10% of adolescent boys and 18% of adolescent girls have made some attempt to take their own life.[8]

♦ 72% of America's teen's have had sexual intercourse by their senior year.[9]

♦ At an average age of 13.2, sexually active high school boys report that they lost their virginity while sexually active girls report an average age of 14.6.[10]

♦ More than one million teenage girls in the United States (one in ten under the age of twenty) become pregnant every year.[11]

♦ 40% of current fourteen-year-old girls will become pregnant at least once before they are twenty![12]

♦ 2.5 million new cases of adolescent sexually transmitted diseases are reported each year.[13]

♦ Nine out of ten teens will have experimented with alcohol by the time they reach their senior year in high school, and 39 percent will get drunk at least once every two weeks.[14]

♦ 19% of all high school seniors report that they initiated cigarette use by the sixth grade.[15]

Men, how did our country go downhill so fast? How did our families crumble before our very eyes? The buck stops with us. Men stopped leading their families in the right direction. As fathers, we are appointed by God to lead our families, but look where we have led them. It's a *disgrace!* Simply put, men have been failing to leave positive spiritual legacies. Men have not walked in wisdom. Men have not redeemed the time.

IS DAD HOME?

According to the Family Research Council, the average father spends only eight minutes a day in direct conversation with his children. In families where the mother works, it drops to four minutes. No wonder many boys suffer from what Robert Bly calls "father hunger"—a longing for a man's love and an insecure sense of masculine identity.

Today, boys spend most of their growing-up years around women—with their mothers at home and female teachers at school and Sunday school. They grow up with only the haziest notion of what their fathers do and, worse, who they are.

Is it *really* important that men are the ones who lead their kids? Yes. When men don't accept the responsibility of investing their time in their kids, look what happens:

♦ 70 percent of juveniles in long-term correctional facilities grew up without a father in the house.
♦ More than 46 percent of the 8.8 million female-headed households with children live in poverty, compared to only 9 percent of the 26.1 million married-couple families with children. Stated differently, fatherless children are five times more likely to live in poverty, compared to children living with both parents.

But a missing father means much more than a missing paycheck. A father's love and discipline are crucial to character formation. And for children growing up without that love, the statistics are grim.

♦ Fatherless children display more *antisocial behavior,* do worse in school, and are twice as likely to drop out than children from intact families.
♦ Fatherless children are more likely to *use drugs* and become *sexually active* at an early age.
♦ More than half the teenagers who have *attempted suicide* live in single-parent homes.

♦ Most children who *run away from home* are leaving fatherless homes.[16]

NOW OR NEVER

Even health rates are affected. A recent study by the Department of Health and Human Services found that after children from broken families are twenty to forty times more likely to suffer health problems than children living with both parents.

The numbers are overwhelming. Our nation can no longer afford to be morally neutral about family forms. For the sake of our children, we must begin to design social policies that support and encourage intact families. David Blankenstorm in *Fatherless America* said, "The most urgent domestic challenge facing the United States at the close of the twentieth century is the re-creation of fatherhood as a vital social role for men."

Which is to say, we need programs that encourage men to take their family responsibilities more seriously. The time has come to shift our attention to the issue of male responsibility and the indispensable role fathers play in family life.

There is a reason God created the family the way He did. Children need fathers as well as mothers in order to thrive. And even more importantly, they need them in order to learn to trust God as their *heavenly* Father.

Dads, *discern the times!* The times are evil. In these days of exceptional evil, are you doing something exceptional?

CHALLENGE #4:
DADS, GROW UP!
So then, do not be foolish but understand what the will of the Lord is.
EPHESIANS 5:17

Men, successful fathering is, not just knowing God's will, but doing it. God has a plan for every family, just as He has a plan for each individual. That plan is called His will and it is the very best God has to offer (Romans 12:2). Home is where a dad is to help his children discover God's will for their lives.

In order for dads to lead their families into God's will, they must first be personally walking in God's will themselves. Dads must *know* the way, *show* the way, and *go* the way.

GROWING IN GRACE

How can we grow in God's will? There are four primary factors that mature us in His will.

First, *God's Word*. God's will is always found within the wisdom and precepts of Scripture. How exactly does the Bible, an ancient book written thousands of years ago, reveal God's way to modern man? There are several key questions we must ask of any passage, the answers to which reveal the way. Is there a command to obey? Is there an example to follow? Is there a promise to claim? Is there a sin to avoid? Is there a principle to follow?

Second, *God's Spirit*. Just as there is the outward objective witness of God's Word, so there is the inward subjective witness of the Holy Spirit. The indwelling Spirit provides guidance into God's perfect will, leading us by the inner witness of His presence. "For all who are being led by the Spirit of God, these are the sons of God" (Romans 8:14, KJV).

Third, *prayer*. God works in response to our prayers when we seek to know His will. The Bible says, "If any of you lacks wisdom, let him ask of God, who gives to all men generously and without reproach, and it will be given to him" (James 1:5, NKJV). Prayer links us with God's heart, allowing us to sense His direction for our lives.

Fourth, *godly counsel*. God leads us into His will through the counsel of other godly people—a spouse, a pastor, a friend, a mentor, a parent, a prayer partner. "Where there is no guidance, the people fall, but in abundance of counselors, there is victory" (Proverbs 11:14). In other words, God steers my life into His will through the wise input of others.

Every father must tap into each of those means of grace—God's Word, God's Spirit, God's face, God's people—in order to discern and follow God's will. Only to the extent that we are walking in God's will are we able to have an impact on our children for eternity.

It is critically important that we begin today with this responsibility of preparing a legacy for our children. The best preparation for tomorrow is the right use of today. Time is more valuable than money because time is irreplaceable. Let us begin *today* because they'll be gone before you know it!

YOU ONLY GET ONE SHOT!

A couple of years ago, I was playing golf with my twin boys, Andrew and James. There was hardly anybody else on the course. We were just having a great time walking down the fairways and talking about various things that fathers and sons talk about.

As we approached our tee shots on one hole, Andrew asked me, "Dad, what do you think is the most important shot in golf?"

I thought, "Now there's a profound question that needs to be answered." But I wanted to hear from him first. So, I countered, "What do *you* think, Buddy?"

In typical fashion, James jumped in and answered before Andrew could even open his mouth. He said, "Dad, Harvey Penick says that the putter is the most important club in the bag. You use the putter more than any other club."

Andrew rebutted, "No, no, Dad. Ben Hogan said it's the driver because it sets up the entire hole. Every other shot is determined by the driver."

I knew what was going on in their minds. I could see the wheels turning inside their heads. They wanted to know on which shot to try their hardest. When should they really bear down? As we put our bags down on the fairway, they began calculating yardage for their club selection, when I made a far more important calculation.

"Boys," I said, "let me tell you what is the most important shot in golf."

With that bold statement, they both stopped dead in their tracks and looked straight up at me. I rested my hands on each boy's shoulder and told them, "Guys, the most important shot in golf is always *your next shot.* You can't be looking back to your last shot. Nor can you be looking ahead to the next hole. The most important shot is always the shot *immediately before you.*"

Dads, the same is true for us. The most important shot that we'll ever have as a father is our very next shot at home. By that, I mean those present opportunities which God provides where we can have an impact on our children—those that are right before us. We must focus upon the shot that is immediately before us and, by the grace of God, leave a spiritual legacy of core values that will have an impact on our children's lives for years to come.

Men, you only get one shot at being a dad.

Make it count!

PART 2

BUILDING
A LEGACY

CHAPTER 3

HOW TO HIT
A HOME RUN AT HOME

A Legacy of Godliness

THE APPLE NEVER FALLS FAR FROM THE TREE.

—Anonymous

The big, bold headlines of the *Sports Illustrated* cover story reached out and grabbed me, and wouldn't let go. The title read, "*MICKEY MANTLE: The Legacy of the Last Great Player on the Last Great Team.*"

Indeed, "The Mick" had left an enormous legacy to the game of baseball. He had been Mr. Baseball to an entire generation. The Tape Measure Kid. The Bronx Bomber. No. 7 in those immortal Yankee pinstripes.

But Mickey Mantle was now *dead*.

As 2,000 well-wishers gathered on August 15, 1995 at Lovers Lane United Methodist Church in Dallas, Texas, the nation mourned the tragic loss of unarguably the most popular and adored athlete of our time. For our sports-crazed nation, Mickey Mantle was its greatest baseball superstar, an American icon who loomed larger than life. Millions of young boys grew up wearing Mickey's No. 7 on their Little League jerseys, dreaming of one day becoming just like their enshrined hero.

But unknown to his admiring fans, this young, blossoming superstar was being driven to self-destructive alcoholism and a life of regrets. On the field, he was America's perennial M.V.P. But off the field, he was becoming crude and obscene through the influence of bar-hopping teammates. He was growing into a wayward husband and distant father, ignoring his wife Merlyn, and four sons Mickey Jr., David, Billy, and Danny.

In the end, Mantle painfully admitted, "I always felt like I wasn't there for my kids."

Under his direct influence, two of his sons became alcoholics, one entering the Betty Ford Center for treatment. "When they were old enough," Mantle confessed, "we became drinking buddies." Tragically, another son died at age thirty-six of an addiction to painkilling drugs. "If I'd gone to Betty Ford sooner, Billy might still be here," a guilt-ridden Mantle lamented. "If I hadn't been drinking, I might have been able to keep him off drugs."[1]

Idolized by millions, The Mick struck out at home.

In the end, Mantle sought to change his life—and did. But by then, it was too late to undo the years of destructive influence upon his family.

Days after his death, the cover of another magazine, *People Magazine,* arrested my attention. In bold, block letters, the headline read, *"THE PRIVATE MICKEY MANTLE: He Played Hard and Lived Harder, Often at his Family's Expense."*[2] On the glossy cover was the full face picture of a young, handsome, twenty-four-year-old Mantle, possessed with explosive athletic ability and superstar potential.

But in the lower left-hand corner was a second photograph. A small insert on the cover portrayed the bitter ending of Mantle's premature death. Here was the sobering picture of his casket being carried into the sanctuary by his pallbearers representing his old life.

The stark contrast between these two pictures spoke volumes about Mantle's two lasting legacies. One photo showed a young superstar with a bright future before him, ready to leave his mark on the game for generations to come. But the other picture revealed this famous father being carried in a casket, having squandered the most important legacy he could have ever left.

His place in history as a baseball player was secure, his legacy as a father was forever *lost.*

It All Starts Here

Leaving a spiritual legacy begins with the personal character of every dad. Who we are determines what we leave behind. By and large, godly children come from godly parents. Certainly there are exceptions. By His saving power, there are children saved out of godless homes to become trophies of His grace. But for the most part, *godly* children come out of *godly* homes where *godly* fathers live *godly* lives. Because like produces like.

If Jesus Christ is to be real in the lives of our children, then He must *first* be real in our own lives. We cannot *leave* what we do not *live*. We cannot *pass on* what we do not *possess*. In fathering, the primary issue is always our own *character*. Who we *are* is more important than what we *do*. Fathering begins deep within ourselves with our own daily walk with God. In a word, it begins with *godliness*.

The most important question any father can ask himself is, "Am I living a godly life? How can I be more godly?"

Here's how to hit a home run at home. Mickey Mantle struck out. But you and I don't have to. If we will live a godly life, we can leave a godly legacy.

With this in mind, I want us to look at Ephesians 5:18–21 in order to discover what marks of godliness must be present in our lives if we are to leave a legacy that lasts. The greatest thing any dad can do for his kids is to be a spiritual man.

FOUNDATION #1:
DADS, BE SPIRIT-FILLED!

*Do not get drunk with wine for that is
dissipation; but be filled with the Spirit.*
EPHESIANS 5:18

First, any father who leaves a legacy that lasts must have a personal relationship with Jesus Christ and be filled with the Holy Spirit. The experience of the new birth radically altars the direction of any man's life. At conversion, the Holy Spirit comes to live permanently inside every believer, never to leave. Only God's Spirit can empower us to be the men He wants us to be. None of us can be an effective father in our own strength. In order for this to be real, Jesus Christ must be the undisputed Lord of our life. And, I might add, we can't fake this at home. Our kids can spot a phony a mile off.

What does it mean to be Spirit-filled?

The word "filled," (Greek word, *pleroo),* means "to be controlled by, to be dominated by, to be under the influence of." The concept of filling does not picture a glass being filled up with water, as if being filled with the Spirit means obtaining more of Him. We received all of the Holy Spirit we will ever have the moment we were saved. God doesn't come in installments. To be Spirit-filled doesn't mean we get more of the Holy Spirit. Rather, the Holy Spirit gets more of us. As we yield our lives to the Holy Spirit, He fills us with the fullness of His presence and He controls, guides, and energizes us.

Don't miss the fact that the apostle Paul is making a deliberate contrast here. The text has two parts—one negative; one positive. Negatively, he says, "don't get drunk." Positively, he says, "Be filled with the Spirit." The Bible is making a purposeful comparison. Being drunk with wine is much like being filled with the Spirit. Just as a drunk man is said to be under the influence of alcohol, so those who are filled with the Spirit come under the influence of the living God. When a person is drunk with wine, he acts "out of character." He *says* things he doesn't normally say. He *does* things he doesn't normally do. He acts with a strange, new boldness.

In just the same way, when a man is filled with the Holy Spirit, he comes under the influence of God. He, too, acts "out of character." His own personality becomes God-like, or godly. He *says* things he doesn't normally say. He *does* things he normally doesn't do. A Spirit-filled person is under the direct influence of Jesus Christ and lives supernaturally.

NOT AN OPTION

Dads, being Spirit-filled is *not* an option. It is a divine command requiring our absolute obedience. At any given moment, we are either controlled by the Holy Spirit or by our flesh (Galatians 5:16). Consequently, our homes are either a little bit of heaven or a little bit of hell, depending upon what influence is leading us, but rarely anything in between. When we are carnal, our families are marked by disputes, anger, arguments, selfishness, impatience, and intolerance (Galatians 5:19–21). But when we are controlled by, filled with the Spirit, our families are marked by the fruit of the Spirit—love, joy, peace, patience, kindness, goodness, faithfulness, gentleness, and self-control (Galatians 5:22–23).

The pivotal question is, Who is controlling us? self? Or the spirit?

The filling of the Spirit is not a one-time experience, but an ongoing experience. We must be *always* filled with the Spirit. God's command to be Spirit-filled is in the present tense, challenging us to *"always be being* filled with the Spirit." We must live every moment of every day, yielded to the Spirit, constantly empowered to be a godly father.

LIKE FATHER, LIKE SON

This is critically important because our children are imitating us more than we realize. *Our* speech, *our* actions, *our* priorities, *our* interests are all being mimicked by our kids and ingrained in their lives.

I remember a television commercial a few years ago that showed a father and a son together. No matter what the father did, the son was standing in the background watching and imitating his dad. The first scenes were cute and innocent, as the father would stand in front of the mirror and comb his hair prompting the son to do likewise. The father would put on his overcoat and walk out the door. Then, sure enough, the son would do the same. Various other acts were copied by the impressionable son.

But the commercial ended in a powerful punch. In the last scene, the father lit up a cigarette and puffed it, not thinking little eyes were watching. The final scene showed the son, as would be expected, peering into a pack of cigarettes and then looking up at his dad. It concluded with the announcer sending a warning, "Like father, like son. Think about it!"

Men, is it any coincidence that our children copy so much about us? Is it by accident that they root for the same football team we do? Is it by happenstance that they react to unexpected interruptions as we do? Is it coincidence that they assume many of our preferences, our likes, and our dislikes? Not hardly.

You've heard the saying, "Your actions scream so loudly, I can't hear a single word you're saying." And, "Actions speak louder than words." How *especially* true in fathering! Unquestionably, our lives will be the most powerful sermon they will ever see or hear.

Howard Hendricks, one of my professors at Dallas Seminary years ago, told us a story one day in class that I've never forgotten. He told us about twin boys who were former students who stopped by his office after class one day to talk. During the course of that conversation, Hendricks asked them about their father, a prominent Christian leader, "Guys, what do you remember most about your dad as you were growing up?"

After a short pause, one of the young men said, "I'll never forget the times he would spend wrestling with us on the floor. Even as teenagers, he would clear out the den furniture and roll around on the floor laughing with us."

The other son reflected, "What I remember most about my dad was, when we were in high school, I threw a paper route and I would have to get up early in the morning to deliver the paper. Each morning, I'd walk past my dad's bedroom door and it would be cracked open. I'd see him in there down on his knees and I knew he was praying for us. That's what I remember most about my dad."

Then "Prof" Hendricks delivered the punch. He leaned across the podium, peered over the top of his glasses, and asked the penetrating question, "By the way, what will your kids remember you for?"

What they remember about us is, more or less, the sum total of the spiritual legacy that we leave behind. Effective fathering begins with our godly character, and such maturity requires that we be Spirit-filled.

But there's more. A Spirit-filled dad will be a singing dad.

FOUNDATION #2:
DADS, BE SINGING!

Speaking to one another in psalms and
hymns and spiritual songs, singing and
making melody with your heart to the Lord.
EPHESIANS 5:19

A godly dad will be a worshiper of the true God who transforms his home into a cathedral of praise. His house will be a place where God is glorified. When God's Spirit controls us, He puts a new song in our hearts, causing us to overflow with praise for Him. A Spirit-filled dad will be known by the praise heard coming from his lips. As the spiritual leader of his home, only a Spirit-controlled dad can be the family worship leader.

Fathers have always been recognized as the priestly worship leaders of their own homes. In ancient days, Abraham built an altar wherever the Lord led him in the Promised Land (Genesis 12:7,8; 13:4,18). Likewise, Job, a contemporary of the patriarchs, built an altar and offered sacrifices on behalf of his children (Job 1:5). When God gave the Law to Moses, He required the fathers of Israel to teach their family His Word in their homes (Deut. 6:5–9). In the book of Proverbs, dad is presented as the primary teacher of God's wisdom in the home (Proverbs 1–9). Deep within the recesses of their hearts, godly dads possess a burning, passionate love for Jesus Christ. Their lives are clearly marked with a fervent faith in God. Praise is ever on their lips.

In Ephesians 5:19, Paul notes that the Spirit-filled dad will express his devotion to God through three chief channels—psalms, hymns, and spiritual songs. Psalms refers directly to the psalter, the 150 psalms of the Bible, which served as the worship book for the early believers. Hymns are theology set to music, the singing of sound doctrine. Spiritual songs are what we call today choruses, or songs that take a particular truth and reinforce it over and over by repetitive singing.

Note, each of these expressions of worship—psalms, hymns, and spiritual songs—will be present in the life of the Spirit-filled dad. Balance is always a key. These various styles allow for a rich variety in our adoration of God.

Worship is primary to passing down a godly heritage to our children. Since worship is the ultimate priority of all creation (Psalm 150; John 4:24; Romans 11:36), it must be a vital part of every father's life. God is real in our lives only to the extent that we worship Him.

SPIRITUAL REPRODUCTION

Dad, do you worship God? Do you live a life of praise? Is there a song in your heart to the Lord? Do your kids see this in your life?

Worship is contagious. When our kids see us magnifying the name of God and sense His preeminence in our lives, they will soon want to do the same. It's as much caught as it is taught.

I have several Norman Rockwell paintings hanging in our house, one of which hangs in our children's bathroom for constant reinforcement. It is a picture of a Sunday morning church scene in which a father and his son are worshipping together.

Both are dressed exactly the same—identical gray suits, white shirts, striped navy ties, and white carnations on their lapels. It is clear that this boy is getting his signals from his dad and is following in close step. But there's more.

Most importantly, both are holding a hymnal. As the father holds his hymnal with one hand, he is helping his son turn to the right page with the other hand. With one hand, he worships; with the other, he helps his son do the same. Side by side, they are engaged together in praising God.

This painting speaks volumes. It portrays worship for what it is, vitally important in the life of a father, who in turn is influencing his son to do the same.

Dad, you are the worship leader in your house. When God is real to you, He will become real in the lives of your children. When He is important to you, He will become important to your kids. Such is the powerful influence of any father upon his family.

So, first, we are to be Spirit-filled; then second, singing; third, satisfied or giving thanks for all things to God.

FOUNDATION #3:
DADS, BE SATISFIED!

Always giving thanks for all things in the name of
our Lord Jesus Christ to God, even the Father.
EPHESIANS 5:20

A godly dad will have a thankful heart. Either we will be humbly grateful, or grumbly hateful. One woman was asked "Do you ever wake up grumpy?" To which she replied, "No, I usually let him sleep in." Unfortunately, many homes have an old grump for it's head when it ought to have a man who is ever giving thanks to God.

One day, a mother and her young son were driving down the street when the inquisitive little boy asked, "Mommy, why do the idiots only come out when Daddy drives?" Sometimes, we can overreact, can't we?

Undoubtedly, our attitude is the thermostat that controls the climate at home. When we come home growling, grumbling, and griping, a negative cloud hovers over our house. But if we come home with a grateful heart, the mood at home will be pleasant and positive. We should exude an "attitude of gratitude" that is constantly expressing thanks to God, no matter what our trial at work, or regardless of what has gone wrong at home. We must always demonstrate a thankful spirit before our family.

Paul says we are to offer thanks "for *all* things." In other words, in every circumstance of life—whether it be good or bad—there is the opportunity to see God at work for His glory and for our good. We must always see "Romans 8:28" written over every situation, always believing that God will cause all things to work together for good in every situation.

I am convinced that many children who grow up in Christian homes fail to walk with the Lord in their adult years because they are turned off by the negative Christianity they saw portrayed at home with their father. Unthankful dads are bad advertisements for the Lord. If we are always complaining about the preacher, constantly criticizing a church program, or forever grumbling about so-and-so at church, is it any wonder our children won't have anything to do with the Lord when they grow up? They often reject Christianity, not because Christ is so irrelevant, but because dad was so negative. A sour spirit poisons a legacy of faith.

Sad to say, some kids can never do anything good enough to merit their dad's praise. Their grades are never high enough. Their performance is never good enough. Their appearance is never sharp enough. Their work is never perfect enough. Their manners are never polished enough. As a result, they grow up insecure and unsure of their dad's love.

But when dad is marked by a thankful spirit, Christianity becomes contagious. In such homes, kids can even fail, yet not diminish their dad's positive spirit. When we are constantly offering thanks to the Lord for the good we see in our children, they are drawn to Christ and to us like bees to honey.

I grew up in just such a home and will be forever grateful. My dad constantly affirmed me and always brought out the good in any given situation. As a result, I grew up always believing that I could do whatever God called me to do.

Dad, how do you respond to bad news around your house? When the car breaks down what is your response? When the washing machine stops working? When the lawn mower gives up the ghost? How you respond to life's circumstances communicates volumes to young hearts. More important than your I.Q. is your "G.Q."—your Gratitude Quotient. Have a grateful attitude and your household will catch it.

This leads to Paul's final challenge:

FOUNDATION #4:
DADS, BE SUBMISSIVE!
And be subject to one another in the fear of Christ.
EPHESIANS 5:21

As godly fathers, we must be submissive to the needs of our wife and children. While dads are the spiritual leaders of their homes, they are not to lord it over their family. Rather, we are to live in humble submission to them, considering their interests to be more important than our own.

Clearly, every family member is to be in submission to each other—wives to husbands, husbands to wives, children to parents, parents to children. In what way are fathers to be submissive to their children? Certainly, we are assigned by God a position of authority over their lives. So, how are we to be submissive to them? The answer is, we are to submit our interests to those of our children. While we do not submit ourselves to their authority, we are to be subject to what will most benefit them. Such self-denial will mark every father who is controlled by God's Spirit.

Many dads have a lot of "clout" at the office, ordering people around and directing their departments, but when they come home, they try the same leadership style with their families. Our children are fragile and require great sensitivity. The power and distance that often characterizes work relationships must be replaced with intimacy, humility, and compassion.

Men, God calls us to be servant-leaders at home, men who lay down our lives for our families. That's what it means to be subject to the interests of our family. If we are to be over them in authority, then we must be under them in humility.

I recall with fondness how my father, who was a strict disciplinarian, willingly sacrificed for me. Money was tight at our house, yet more times than not, what little discretionary income we had went for my sports activities rather than for his personal desires. But the greatest way in which he sacrificed for me was the giving of his time. Although my dad kept a busy schedule as a professor in medical school and as a researcher for private pharmaceutical companies, he always made the time to come to my ball games and practices, as well as other activities. His life became subject to my needs and interests.

Men, this is what we must do for our children's needs, sacrificing our preferences for their good. God will use our self-humiliation to prepare their hearts to receive Christ, to walk with Him daily, and to live successfully.

Pass It On!

In this chapter, we have discovered that leaving a godly legacy begins with living a godly life! We can only pass on what has first gripped us. In other words, we cannot impart what we do not possess. We cannot lead where we have not already gone.

I can only lead my family properly to the extent that I am rightly related to God. Every dad must, first, have a right relationship with God before he can have a right relationship with his kids. Every father must first be a follower of Christ before he can be a leader of his children.

Men, has Christ become a present reality in your life? Have you committed your life to Him by faith? Have you believed in your heart that Jesus died on the cross for *your* sins? Have you received Him to be your personal Lord and Savior? And are you walking closely to Him in personal holiness? The greatest thing you can do for your kids is to love Jesus Christ and experience His life-changing power daily.

THAT'S MY DADDY

A little girl once was standing on the edge of a crowd while her daddy was giving a testimony about what Jesus Christ had done in his life. He was testifying how the Lord had saved him and delivered him from his old lifestyle as a drunkard.

There was a cynic standing on the edge of the crowd that day who could not bear to hear anymore of this religious nonsense. So he yelled, "Why don't you shut up and sit down, old man. You're just *dreaming.*"

Soon, this skeptic felt a tug on his coat sleeve. He looked down and it was this little girl. She looked him square in the eyes and said, "Sir, that's my daddy you're talking about. You say that my daddy is a dreamer? Let me tell you about my daddy.

"My daddy used to be a drunkard and would come home at night and beat my mother. She would cry all through the night. And mister, we didn't have good clothes to wear because my daddy spent all his money on whiskey. Sometimes I didn't even have shoes to wear to school. But look at these shoes and look at this dress! My daddy has a good job now."

Then pointing across the way, she said, "Do you see that woman smiling over there? That's my mother. She doesn't cry through the night anymore. Now she sings."

Then the knockout punch. She said, "Jesus has changed my daddy. Jesus has changed our home. Mister, if my daddy is dreaming, *please don't wake him up.*"

Men, the power of God changes our lives too. And when it does, such a transformation will be obvious to our children. When they observe our changed lives, they will want the same.

Let us live a godly life. And as we do, we will leave a godly legacy for our children to possess. Because like produces like.

CHAPTER 4

IT ALL STARTS AT THE TOP

A Legacy of Love

WHEN GOD MEASURES A MAN, HE PUTS THE TAPE
AROUND HIS HEART—NOT HIS HEAD.

—*Anonymous*

Leaving a legacy requires love, and lots of it.

I heard about a wealthy man who traveled the world collecting rare paintings and purchasing treasures of art. He had only one son, a very ordinary boy who grew up in relative obscurity, hardly noticed by others. When he grew to become a young man, he died unexpectedly and his father greatly mourned the loss.

Within a few months after the tragic death, the father died as well from a broken heart, leaving behind his incredible rare art collection. In his will, he stipulated that everything he owned was to be auctioned off. And strangely enough, he requested that one particular painting was to be auctioned first—a portrait of his son done by an unknown artist.

A large crowd assembled and, according to the will, the auctioneer did exactly what was instructed. He first directed their attention to bid upon this portrait of the obscure son of the wealthy man. But no one knew the boy. No one knew the artist, and no one really cared for the painting.

A long time passed without any bid being placed. Until finally, an old black man who had been a servant in the house of the wealthy man came forward. He placed a one dollar bid on the portrait of the son whom he loved very much, that being all he could afford.

There were no other bids, so the black servant was able to purchase the painting of the son for one dollar. Then came the dramatic moment when the auctioneer read the next portion of the will. To the astonishment of everyone, it read, "The entire rest of my vast art collection shall go to the one who loved my son enough to purchase his portrait."

By loving his son, this servant received the entire estate.

That's precisely the way a spiritual legacy works, as well. By loving God's Son, all the vast treasures of God's kingdom are passed down with it. When we love Christ, a rich legacy is left for our children.

But we must do more than love Christ. We must also love the wife God has given us, if a spiritual legacy is to be bequeathed. The greatest thing we can ever do to pass down the legacy to our kids, apart from loving God, is to love their mom.

I love my kids. But the greatest way I can show my love for them, apart from loving God, is loving their mom. Kids need to see love between their parents, and when they do, their hearts are prepared to receive the love of God.

Men, the importance of loving our wives cannot be overstated in passing down a legacy to our children. As they see love, they feel loved. Love between mom and dad is the foundation upon which a lasting legacy is built for our children.

In Ephesians 5:22–23, Paul challenges us to lead our wives and love them as Christ loved the church. That's no small assignment! We must be both a *leader* and a *lover*. This is not an either/or, but a both/and. Both aspects—leading and loving—must be present.

Look at it this way. A leader who does not love his wife is a harsh dictator. And a lover who does not lead her is a spineless wimp. But the husband who is both a leader and a lover is a man who provides the greatest legacy possible for his children. Love must be real between a husband and wife before it can be real between a father and his children. Here's what we must do toward our wives:

CHARGE #1:
DADS, LEAD YOUR WIFE!

Wives, be subject to your own husbands, as to the Lord.
For the husband is the head of the wife, as Christ also is the head of the church,

He Himself being the Savior of the body. But as the church is subject to Christ,
so also the wives ought to be to their husbands in everything.

EPHESIANS 5:22–23

As Paul describes our relationship with our wife, he begins by establishing the headship of the husband over his wife. Clearly, the man is the head of his wife, just as Christ is head of His church. So what does headship mean? In a day when there is great misunderstanding about the role of spiritual leadership in the home by men and the submission of women to their husbands, clear, biblical thinking is needed. In order to provide this, I want us to consider four key words that will help us define the truth about headship. These four words are *equality, authority, responsibility,* and *intimacy.* Let's look at each:

EQUALITY

Whatever we say about the headship of the husband, it comes within the context of equality between a man and his wife. The two sexes have equal status in God's kingdom. Galatians 3:26–28 says, "For you are all sons of God through faith in Christ Jesus. For all of you who were baptized into Christ have clothed yourselves with Christ. There is neither Jew nor Greek, there is neither slave nor free man, there is neither male nor female; for you are all one in Christ Jesus." Because husbands and wives are one in Christ, our difference must be one of function and role, not value or importance.

Unquestionably, wives have equal status with their husbands in God's kingdom. History records that Christianity elevated women to a high standing never before known in the ancient world. While God has assigned men the role of headship, the Bible is equally clear that there is absolutely no distinction between the sexes in the realm of spiritual privilege. So, whatever differences are implied by the headship of the man, there is absolute equality between the two sexes. The ground at the foot of the cross is level.

AUTHORITY

Literally, headship means the right to rule. When Paul says that wives are to be subject to their own husbands (22–24), he uses a Greek word (*hupotasso*) which means "to line up" (*tasso*) "under" (*hupo*). *Hupotasso* means to line up under the authority of another. It was a military word used in the first century describing a soldier lining up under an officer who was placed over him. Therefore, submission means to be under the authority of one placed by God over you.

There is a chain of command designed by God for the home. Paul says in 1 Corinthians 11:3, "But I want you to understand that Christ is the head of every man, and the man is the head of a woman, and God is the head of Christ." This teaches that God is the head of Christ, that Christ is the head of every man, (*anthropos,* meaning both male or female), and that a man (*aner,* meaning male) is the head of his wife. In other words, Christ is the head of all people, male or female, and the man is the head of his wife. The same headship and submission that exists within the Godhead is to exist within the home. Just as Jesus Christ is in submission to the will of His Father, so wives are to be to their husbands.

Theologically, we know that God the Son is co-equal and co-eternal with God the Father. In fact, it would be flaming heresy of the highest order if we said that Jesus Christ was anything less than fully God. Jesus said, "I and the Father are one" (John 10:30), meaning one in the essence of their deity. And the apostle Paul wrote that Jesus "existed in the form of God and thought it not robbery to be equal with God" (Philippians 2:6). The Father and the Son have equal status and joint privilege within the Godhead.

Yet Jesus chose to submit to the will of the Father. He said, "I've come down from heaven, not to do My own will, but the will of Him who sent Me" (John 6:38, NKJV). In like manner, a wife is equal to her husband, yet her husband has authority over her in the Lord.

RESPONSIBILITY

Great authority over our wives brings great responsibility. As the leaders of our homes, we have the God-given responsibility to oversee all the affairs of our family. Of the man who is spiritually mature, the Bible says, "He must be one who manages his own household while keeping his children under control with all dignity" (1 Timothy 3:4). To "manage" means to preside over, to have authority over. The same word is translated "rule" elsewhere (1 Timothy 5:17). In like manner, husbands are to manage well their family, meaning to oversee everything connected with their home, whether it be morals, finances, child rearing, house repairs, or whatever.

INTIMACY

In the analogy of headship, the head is directly connected to the lower body over which it presides. The life of one flows into the life of the other. For the head to function, it must remain closely united to the body. The head must never be detached from the rest of the body. If such a separation occurs, there will be an immediate death and both the head and the body will cease to live. So it is in the marriage relationship. A man's headship implies that he is to live in close intimacy with his wife. If we ever grow distant from our wives, whether emotionally, spiritually, or physically, then a sure death will occur in the relationship and we will both cease to function as God designed.

First Peter 3:7 says, "You husbands likewise, live with your wives in an understanding way, as with a weaker vessel, since she is a woman; and grant her honor as a fellow heir of the grace of life, so that your prayers may not be hindered." We must do more than co-exist with our wives. *We must live together with them.* We should live with our wife with a knowledge of her unique temperament, personality, strengths, weaknesses, and breaking (or boiling) points. Your wife is a one-of-a-kind distinctive creation who is wonderfully different from any other woman God ever made. You must get to know and appreciate her as the subject of your most careful study. Love her accordingly.

For example, some wives can be teased, others can't. Some can adjust to frequent moves, others can't. Some require more listening time than others. Your wife may not be able to cope with unexpected supper guests while others can. Many wives need eight hours of sleep, others less. Some wives are "late-nighters," others are early to bed, early to rise. Every husband must live intimately with his wife and become an expert on her unique personality and needs.

Men, our wives long for us to be intimate with them. When our heart is filled with the Lord we are most likely to be filled with love for our wife. That's because "God is love" (1 John 4:8). This is what women long for—intimate communication—and only the Holy Spirit can give us this kind of sensitivity. This challenge to lead and love our wives underscores our need to be filled with the Holy Spirit.

These same four key words that mark the husband-wife relationship—equality, authority, responsibility and intimacy—should define the father-child parental relationship. What is true of our relationship with our wife should be true with our relationship with our children. How you lead your wife will influence how you love your children.

Each of these four truths is critically important for a comprehensive and balanced understanding of headship. It is like a four-legged table. If you don't have any one of the four legs, the table is unstable and will fall over. So each of these elements are necessary to support our relationship with our wife.

CHARGE #2:
DADS, LOVE YOUR WIFE!

Husbands, love your wives just as Christ also
loved the church and gave Himself up for her.
EPHESIANS 5:25

Every man, as the leader, needs to love his wife in a special way.

Did you hear the one about the wedding ceremony where the minister said, "Do you take this woman for better or for worse? For richer or for poorer? In sickness and in health?" And the groom said, "Yes, no, yes, no, no, yes."

Of course, we'd all like to sign up for the better, richer, and healthier parts when we get married and forget all the other stuff. But that's not the way marriage works because that's not the way life works.

I heard about another wedding ceremony, this one real, during which the bride and groom pledged to stay married as long as they continued to love each other. Well, I hope they both know good divorce attorneys, because they are going to need them.

Relationships based on feelings are necessarily ephemeral and transitory. The only real stability in marriage is produced by firm commitments that hold two people steady when emotions are fluctuating wildly. Without this determination to cement human relationships, they are destined to disintegrate.

Can you imagine a parent saying to the child, "I'll care for you as long as I shall love you?" That would hardly portend stability and well-being for the child. Nor does a wishy-washy expression of love hold much promise for the future of a marriage.

Emotion might be thought of as the caboose on a train. A committed will is the engine that pulls the relationship through all the ups and downs of everyday living.

Leading without loving would be dictatorial. There are several features about this love that requires our attention. Our love is to be:

An Unconditional Love

Paul begins by saying, "Husbands, love your wives…" (Ephesians 5:25). There are three words used in the Greek language for love. The first, *eros,* refers to sexual passion on the physical level. The second, *philo,* is an affectionate friendship and partnership on the emotional level. The third, *agape,* is the unconditional commitment of one person to another which is God-like in nature. Agape love is the kind of love that God has demonstrated toward us in Christ (John 3:16). Not surprisingly, this is the word found in verse 25 here *(agape)* and describes how we are to love our wives—*unconditionally!*

There are no qualifiers or disclaimers. There are no exceptions or escape clauses to this kind of love. *Agape* love is a choice of the will, not a feeling of the emotions. We are to love our wife whether she is deserving or not. How unlike the so-called love we hear talked about in the world. The world's love is always driven by the physical attractiveness, witty personality, or popular prestige of the one loved. In other words, the world loves those whom it deems worthy of its love. But such love is not really love and is foreign to what God requires of a man toward his wife.

God calls us to unconditionally accept our wife because He is the one who brought her to us! Our unconditional acceptance of our wife is based upon our belief in the holy character and sovereign choice of God. If we believe that God wisely selected our wife and sovereignly brought her to us, then we will accept her as a gift from the Lord. To refuse her is to refuse the Lord.

This was the basis for Adam's acceptance of Eve. Because he trusted God, he could receive his wife. Scripture records that Adam received Eve, but not because of any prior knowledge that he had of her. He had never met her in his life. It was not because he had had a previous date with her. It was not because of her cooking. Rather Adam's acceptance of her was based upon his absolute trust in the character of God.

Bottom line, men, we must unconditionally love and accept our wives. Because we believe God sovereignly brought her to us, our acceptance of her is a reflection of our acceptance of God's guidance in our lives. She is a helpmate uniquely designed, or tailor-made, for us (Genesis 2:18). Proverbs 19:14 says, "House and wealth are an inheritance from fathers, but a prudent wife is from the Lord." In other words, your father may give you an earthly legacy, but only God can bring you a priceless treasure like your wife.

Proverbs 31:10 says, "An excellent wife, who can find?" It is a rhetorical question implying a negative answer. If you were to search all your life, you could never find such an excellent wife as yours. Only God can bring her to you. Now that He has, receive her and love her.

An Unreserved Love

The apostle Paul continues to describe the kind of love we are to give our wives when he writes, "Just as Christ also loved the church and gave Himself up for her" (Ephesians 5:25b). At the cross, Christ demonstrated the supreme act of love when He laid down His life for us. "Greater love has no man than this, than one lay down his life for his friends" (John 15:13). Here was the ultimate sacrifice—He loved us unto death, even the horrible death of a cross. Christ gave up His comfort and conveniences, His rights and riches, because He loved us. He gave up being served day and night in heaven by the angels in order to become a bond-servant and serve us on earth. "He was rich, yet for your sake He became poor, that you through His poverty might become rich" (2 Corinthians 8:9). Our salvation came at an enormous price. It cost Jesus *everything!*

Men, this is how we are to love our wives. We must love them with a sacrificial love, willingly yielding our pleasures and preferences, choosing to give up our comforts and conveniences. Rather than being served, God calls us to sacrifice for our wives—whatever the cost! True love is all about *giving,* not *getting.* This cuts against the very grain of our male ego which desires to be catered to and pampered.

An Undefiled Love

Love wants only the best for the one loved. Paul writes:

> That He might sanctify her, having cleansed her by the washing of water with the word, that He might present to Himself the church in all her glory, having no spot or wrinkle or any such thing; but that she should be holy and blameless. (Ephesians 5:26–27)

It will never defile the one loved, nor allow her to be corrupted by anything evil or harmful. Consequently, our love will seek to protect our wives from the world's pollution and shield them from all that would contaminate them.

To sanctify means to set something or someone apart to a particular use or influence. Usually, the word signifies setting apart something to purity or godliness. For Christ to sanctify His bride, the church, means that He sets us apart from the pollution of sin so that we might become holy and pure like Himself. His love for us is undefiled. He will never tempt us or lead us into sin.

Men, this is how we are to love our wives. We are to love them with a purifying love which protects them from the defiling influences of the world. We will be careful where we take our wives, what we say to them, and what influences to which we allow them to be exposed. At the same time, we must provide them with an environment where the Word of God will purify their lives. One day Christ will present Himself to the church without spot or blemish. In like manner, we are responsible to provide a spiritual atmosphere for our wives so they can grow in the grace and knowledge of God.

At home, we must nurture our wives spiritually, praying with them, praying for them, speaking God's Word, helping discern God's will, and offering words of encouragement. Also, this requires finding a church where they can grow spiritually, and then attending regularly together.

An Understanding Love

In the marriage relationship, the husband and the wife become one in the Lord, or "one flesh" as verse 31 says. Paul writes,

> So husbands ought also to love their own wives as their own bodies. He who loves his own wife loves himself; for no one ever hated his own flesh, but nourishes and cherishes it, just as Christ also does the church, because we are members of His body. (Ephesians 5:28–30)

The man who loves his wife is actually loving himself because the two are one. No one hates his own body. When I am hungry, I feed my body. When I am tired, I rest my body. When I am hurt, I care for my body. I am most aware of my own personal needs and am committed to attending to those needs. That's how I am to love my wife. I'm to be as aware of her needs as I am of my own body. And I'm to be just as committed to meeting her needs as I am to meeting those needs of my own body. When I please her, I am pleasing myself. When I am hurting her, I am hurting myself.

Similarly, when my wife hurts, I am to know it, feel it, and respond to her. When she is overloaded and discouraged, then I must respond to her need. When she is pulled in every direction, I am to come alongside and help. Also, when she rejoices, I am to share her joy as well. That's how sensitive I am to be in my love toward her. But unfortunately, we're not always as sensitive as we ought to be. Sometimes we grow more callous toward our wives the longer that we are with them.

My kids picked out this Mother's Day card to give to Anne. On the front of the card it says, "Just for you on Mother's Day... Relax, put your feet up, have some coffee and have some tea, read the paper, watch TV, don't cook, don't clean, don't wash, don't iron, just do what makes you glad. In other words, for this one day..." Then you open it up and on the inside it says, "...just pretend you're Dad."

I don't know why my kids picked that particular card.

Several years ago, the Saturday Evening Post published an article entitled "The Seven Stages of the Married Cold." It revealed the reaction of a husband to his wife's colds during their first seven years of marriage. It went something like this:

The first year: "Sugar dumpling, I'm really worried about my baby girl. You've got a bad sniffle, and there's no telling about these things with all this strep throat going around. I'm putting you in the hospital this afternoon for a general checkup and a good rest. I know the food's lousy, but I'll be bringing your meals in from Rossini's. I've already got it all arranged with the floor superintendent."

The second year: "Listen, darling, I don't like the sound of that cough. I called Doc Miller and asked him to rush over here. Now you go to bed like a good girl, please? Just for papa."

The third year: "Maybe you'd better lie down, honey; nothing like a little rest when you feel lousy. I'll bring you something to eat. Have you got any canned soup?"

The fourth year: "Now look, dear, be sensible. After you've fed the kids, washed the dishes, and finished the floor, you'd better lie down."

The fifth year: "Why don't you take a couple of aspirin?"

The sixth year: "I wish you'd just gargle or something, instead of sitting around all evening barking like a seal!"

The seventh year: "For Pete's sake, stop sneezing! Are you trying to give me pneumonia?"[1]

That's the decline of marriage as seen through the common cold. A funny look at a not-so-funny reality.

Without a doubt, God calls us to love our wives with sensitivity and self-lessness. We must be so in touch with their needs that it's as if we were loving our own body.

An Unending Love

In a day of disposable marriages with optional escape clauses, God calls husbands to love their wives with an unbreakable, unending love. Certainly this is how Christ loves the church, for nothing shall ever separate us from the love of Christ. The apostle writes:

> For this cause a man shall leave his father and mother, and shall cleave to his wife; and the two shall become one flesh. (Ephesians 5:31)

When we become married, we must leave behind our one-time allegiance and loyalty to our parents in order to establish a new primary relationship with our wife. There must be a leaving before there can be a cleaving. There must be a severance before there can be a joining.

The word "cleave" (*proskollao*) means, literally, to glue or weld something permanently together. Husbands are to be permanently cemented to their wives. This means that divorce is to be avoided at all costs. God hates divorce (Matthew 2:16). He will tolerate it in only two instances—adultery and abandonment—but he still hates it. God calls us to work through each and every difference and dispute with our wife because "what God has joined together, let no man separate" (Matthew 19:6).

An Uncommon Love

Finally, the relationship that exists between us and our wife illustrates the love which exists between Christ, the bridegroom; and the church, His bride.

This mystery is great; but I am speaking with reference to Christ and the church. Nevertheless let each individual among you also love his own wife even as himself; and let the wife see to it that she respects her husband. (Ephesians 5:32–33)

Here lies one of the reasons—if not *the* greatest reason—our marriage is so important—because God's honor and reputation is at stake in our marriage. These verses elevate the husband-wife relationship to a sacred level because it pictures the relationship between Christ and His church.

As Christian men, we are called to love all people, even our enemies. But this passage sets apart the unique love that we should have for our wife. At stake is a vivid portrayal and a living picture of the mystical union between Christ and His bride, the church.

Think about the implications of this truth. We must avoid divorce at all costs, not simply for selfish reasons, but for God's reputation. We must have a sense of fear that we properly love our wives because God sees this as more than a mere partnership—but a reflection of who He is in the world. Uniquely, the husband-wife relationship mirrors the image and glory of God (Genesis 1:26–27).

The eternal importance and spiritual significance placed upon marriage far outweighs any other earthly relationship. The eternal is at stake, not merely the earthly. Bad Christian marriages create barriers for the unbelieving world to come to Christ. But Christ-centered marriages where the husband both leads and loves his wife as Christ does the church draws unbelievers to the reality of Christ and the difference He can make in a marriage.

How do we love our wives? Unconditionally, sacrificially, with a purifying love, with sensitivity, that is a permanent sacred love.

BACK ON THE RIGHT TRACK

Some time ago, I had become so busy in serving the church, and so preoccupied with our kids, that I was neglecting my wife, Anne. My life was too busy to be the husband I should have been for her. It was rise early, sprint to the office, study for sermons, return phone calls, dash home, play with our kids, eat dinner, help with their homework, do their baths, put them to bed, then collapse. Day after day. Week after week. Month after month.

I felt myself too exhausted to talk to Anne. Even when I tried to talk to her, I didn't have the emotional energy to pour myself into it. On top of that, there was always a distraction. The phone would ring. The doorbell would ring. The kids would cry. The church would call.

I had to do something. So, I bought two train tickets, just for the two of us to be together.

My plan was to board the train and then, for seven uninterrupted hours, just be alone and talk. Just us. No committee meetings. No counseling. No kids. No telephone calls. No books. No emergencies. No interruptions.

Just Anne and me.

Alone.

When we boarded the train, we had the entire passenger car to ourselves! As the train pulled out of the station, we hardly knew what to say to each other, what with no children interrupting us! We just stared at each other. Then out the window. Then back at each other.

But small talk soon became intimate talk. Here was the woman I married. It had been so long since we had had a quiet moment like this. This was just what our relationship needed. A second honeymoon. Just the two of us. And our relationship was back on track

Men, the greatest thing we can do for our kids, apart from loving God, is to love our wives. Nothing else on a horizontal plane even comes close. Our children need to see us loving our wife, and when they do, a door is opened to their heart allowing us entrance into their lives.

Here is the real measure of a man.

CHAPTER 5

PREPARING A WILL BEFORE IT'S TOO LATE

A Legacy of Obedience

THE THING THAT IMPRESSES ME MOST ABOUT AMERICA
IS THE WAY PARENTS OBEY THEIR CHILDREN.
—*Duke of Windsor*

Not every legacy passed down by a father is successfully received by the next generation. Some are lost in the transfer.

Not long ago, a financial counselor showed me a case study of large estates left behind by famous celebrities after their death. These highly visible personalities from the world of entertainment, politics, and commerce were grouped according to the amount of wealth they bequeathed to their heirs. Here's what I discovered.

- ♦ **$500,000 to $2,000,000** estates included names like Jimmy Durante, Harry Truman, Robert F. Kennedy, and Humphrey Bogart.
- ♦ **$2,000,000 to $5,000,000** estates had such notables as Clark Gable, Dwight D. Eisenhower, Henry Fonda, and Gary Cooper.
- ♦ **$5,000,000 to $10,000,000** estates listed famous personalities as Yul Brynner, Jack Benny, Cole Porter, and William Holden.
- ♦ **$10,000,000 to $15,000,000** estates boasted celebrities like Elvis Presley among others.
- ♦ **$15,000,000 to $25,000,000** estates had luminous names like J.P. Morgan, Walt Disney, and Alfred Hitchcock.

- ♦ **$25,000,000 to $50,000,000** estates contained names like John D. Rockefeller, Sr., and Samuel Goldwyn.
- ♦ **$50,000,000** estates and more had business giants like William Randolph Hearst, Nelson Rockefeller, John D. Rockefeller, and Conrad Hilton.[1]

In each case, there is listed the gross amount of the celebrity's estate, followed by the actual amount of money lost in the transfer to their beneficiaries. This reduction, called a shrinkage percentage, is the total amount lost to the deceased: outstanding debts, attorney's fees, executor's fees, inheritance taxes, estate taxes, and administrative taxes. After death, all these expenses are subtracted from the gross value of the estate.

Interestingly enough, not everyone's shrinkage percentage was the same. In fact, they weren't even close.

The person with the *largest* shrinkage percentage was the legendary Elvis Presley. At his death, the King of Rock 'n' Roll left a legacy of over $10,000,000. But, after his estate was settled, more than $7,000,000 was deducted, leaving a staggering loss of 73 percent! Only $2,700,000 was passed on to his heirs. No wonder he was all shook up! The greatest portion of Elvis's inheritance was never seen by his descendants.

On the other hand, other famous personalities managed to see their estate transfer safely to their children with a relatively small shrinkage percentage. For example, the estate of Henry Fonda, valued at over $4,000,000 at the time of his death, saw a mere $33,045 lost in settling costs, a small fraction of the whole. While Elvis Presley lost 73 percent of his legacy, Henry Fonda lost less than 1 percent. Although the Presley estate had more money, Fonda heirs actually inherited more.

Why was a large proportion of some estates lost?

The answer is simple—*it got lost in the transfer.* Better to leave a relatively small estate that transfers safely than to bequeath a large one that becomes lost in the transfer. It's one thing to pass down a great fortune, but something else entirely to see it received by your heirs without significant loss.

Men, what's true in finances is true in fathering. It's one thing for us to personally possess the abundant riches of Jesus Christ. But it's something else entirely to see them passed safely to our children without being lost in the transfer.

Leaving such a spiritual legacy, as we have seen in the last two chapters, requires leaving a legacy of godliness and love. And it also requires, as we shall see in this chapter, leaving a legacy of obedience. We must prepare their will.

PREPARING A WILL "NOW"!

My wife Anne had been urging me for years that we needed to prepare a will. But being the procrastinator that I am, I kept putting if off until I finally gave in and set up an appointment with a lawyer.

As I sat there in his office, I began to mentally itemize all my valuable possessions that would one day pass down to my kids. Golf clubs. Baseball cards. Electric train set. Ping-Pong table. Hardly the kind of assets to have rivaled the estates of Elvis Presley or the Rockefellers.

I remember feeling a great sense of relief when I signed the last line of the will. Now, I had the peace of mind knowing that all my earthly posses-sions would not go to the government, nor be absorbed by state institutions. Rather my estate would go to those whom I love the most—my family.

All in all, it was a fairly painless procedure. Several hours of my time and a few hundred dollars. Hopefully, I'll never have to prepare a will again, except for occasional revisions.

However, there is *another kind of will* that I'm still in the process of preparing. It's one that takes more than a few hours to prepare. One that costs more than a few hundred dollars. I'm talking about the will that resides deep within the heart of your children—their will to *choose,* their will to *decide,* their will to *sort out* and *select.* That's the will every father must prepare before it's too late.

Whether you have a strong-willed child, or a compliant child, it is our responsibility to capture their will as soon as possible and bring it into sub-mission to our authority, as well as ultimately, to God's authority. We must prepare their will *now* while it is young and pliable so that they will choose what God intends for them to have.

These truths are about how to be the parent of a godly child. And at the heart of a godly child is a will that obeys the Lord. Now, I must warn you. If your main objective is to be the parent of a *rich* and *famous* child, these truths are not for you. If your number one goal is to be the parent of a *popular* child, then principles on etiquette might be more appropriate here. Now please understand, no one wants his child to grow up to be a failure in the world, nor become a social nerd. That's not my point here. If your driving desire is to be the parent of a *godly* child, these truths are for you.

I find today, even among many Christians, an overwhelming desire for their kids to become as much like the world as they possibly can. All too often, these well-meaning parents want their children to so merge with and blend into the world that, I believe, they lose their distinctiveness as Christians.

Bottom line, our children must be different if they're going to make a difference. If our children are to be different, then our parenting must be different. It's always been this way. Way back in the Old Testament, God called the people of God to be different from the world. He said:

> You shall not do what is done in the land of Egypt where you live, nor are you to do what is done in the land of Canaan where I am bringing you; you shall not walk in their statutes. You are to perform My judgments and keep My statutes to live in accord with them; I am the Lord, your God. You shall keep My statutes and My judgments by which a man may live if he does them; I am the Lord. (Leviticus 18:3–4)

The same principle applies to our parenting. God says, "Don't raise your children to be like the Egyptians. Don't raise them to be like the Canaanites. I have called you out of Egypt to bring you into a new way of living. Follow my Word and be different from the world." When God says "different," He doesn't mean weird. Some Christians are odd, but not different. What God is talking about is a different set of values for your family—God's values—so that your children stand out in the world.

A MATTER OF THE WILL

At the very heart of this difference is the fact that your children should posses a will which acts in obedience to authority. Obedience is a core virtue that we must instill within our children. A spirit of rebellion and anarchy lives in the world all around us. If we can teach obedience to our children, they will be positioned to excel in all that they do in life. All of life is dependent upon obedience to authority.

If children are to function successfully in society, they must learn to be in submission to their employers, teachers, coaches, scout leaders, as well as to law and government officials. If a child can learn to be obedient at home toward his parents, then he will be obedient in the other important areas of his life. Obedience is a lifestyle.

For example, I came to faith in Christ early in life, I believe, because my father taught me to obey him at a young age. He brought my will into submission to his authority. Therefore, it became a natural thing for me to submit to God's authority. Obedience was a lifestyle which then carried over to other areas of my life—sports, school, church, and the like. Obedience to my father shaped my entire life and helped me to be successful wherever I found myself in society.

Dads, that is what we want to do. We want to prepare a will before it's too late—the will of our children.

First, a word of review. We have already laid a strong foundation in our relationship with God (Ephesians 5:15–21) and our wife (Ephesians 5:22–33). Only when these two relationships are right can we be prepared to be the father to our children that God calls us to be. So being right with God and right with your wife, leads to being right with your children. In other words, we must be obedient ourselves before we can *teach* obedience. That makes sense, doesn't it?

Let's zero in on Ephesians 6:1 now and learn how we can lead our children to live in obedience. Here are the four essential responsibilities of every father who wants to leave a legacy of obedience. We must *demand* it, *define* it, *develop* it, and *demonstrate* it.

RESPONSIBILITY #1:
DADS, DEMAND OBEDIENCE!

Children, obey your parents in the Lord, for this is right.
EPHESIANS 6:1

Men, obedience in the lives of our kids begins by requiring it of them. In this verse, God calls all children to obey their parents. But before our children can obey us, as this verse so clearly says, this presupposes that we must take the initiative to teach them to obey. As Paul speaks to children here, he is speaking to fathers, as well, to cultivate such obedience.

Why must we teach our children to obey us?

Because every child is born with a sin nature, a predisposition bent toward disobedience. Yes, that precious little child of yours was born with—I hope that you're sitting down for this—an evil heart. The Bible says, "The heart is more deceitful than all else and is desperately sick, who can understand it?" (Jeremiah 17:9). That sinful heart must be conquered and brought into a place of humble submission before it will obey.

Take, for example, our precious daughter Grace Anne who could do no wrong. Or so I thought. When she was twenty months of age, she spied a candlestick in the living room that she was determined to have. After being told not to touch it, eight consecutive times, she removed the candlestick and took it off with her. And subsequently, eight consecutive times she received a spanking on her hands. Even in the heart of the most precious little child, there is a bent toward sin.

Why is that? The Bible teaches that we all came into this world with a sin nature that is in rebellion against God. The psalmist said, "Behold, I was brought forth in iniquity, and in sin my mother conceived me" (Psalms 51:5). Again, he wrote, "The wicked are estranged from the womb; these who speak lies go astray from birth" (Psalm 58:3). All children—my children, your children—inherited this sin nature at the moment of conception and stepped out of their mother's womb going down the wrong path away from God.

Now before you get too hard on them, understand this, men—they got their sin nature from *you*.

Leaving no room for doubt, the apostle Paul lumps all mankind together and concludes that *all*—not just adults, but children, also—are under the guilt and power of sin when he writes:

Both Jews and Greeks are all under sin; as it is written, THERE IS NONE RIGHTEOUS, NOT EVEN ONE; THERE IS NONE WHO UNDERSTANDS, THERE IS NONE WHO SEEKS FOR GOD; ALL HAVE TURNED ASIDE, TOGETHER THEY HAVE BECOME USELESS; THERE IS NONE WHO DOES GOOD, THERE IS NOT EVEN ONE. THEIR THROAT IS AN OPEN GRAVE, WITH THEIR TONGUES THEY KEEP DECEIVING, THE POISON OF ASPS IS UNDER THEIR LIPS; WHOSE MOUTH IS FULL OF CURSING AND BITTERNESS; THEIR FEET ARE SWIFT TO SHED BLOOD, DESTRUCTION AND MISERY ARE IN THEIR PATHS, AND THE PATH OF PEACE HAVE THEY NOT KNOWN. THERE IS NO FEAR OF GOD BEFORE THEIR EYES. (Romans 3:9–18)

That's not a pretty picture, is it? This indictment of the entire human race teaches that every person is born with total depravity. That means a sin nature that extends to their total humanity—their mouth, their heart, their eyes, their feet. From the top of their head, (referring to their life thoughts), to the bottom of their feet, (referring to their activities), they're totally depraved. That includes all mankind—you, me, and our children.

How did we get into such a mess?

THE FIRST DAD

The Bible traces this problem back to the first man, Adam. His original sin was like a drop of cyanide poison released into a glass of water, immediately spreading and poisoning the entire contents. In just that same way, when Adam sinned, his sin spread to the entire human race. The apostle Paul wrote, "Therefore, just as through one man sin entered into the world, and death through sin, and so death spread to all men because all sinned" (Romans 5:12–14). After Adam sinned, he—as well as every subsequent father—could only beget children with a sin nature. God created Adam in His own image (Genesis 5:1–2), but after Adam sinned, he produced children in his own sinful image (verse 3). Like produces like. Sinful fathers produce sinful children.

Dad, your child has a heart problem! He or she was born into this world with a sin nature inherited from you! The sin nature is transmitted through the male! That's why Jesus had to be born of a virgin without a human father so that He would not have an inherited sin nature. But, unfortunately, our children are not virgin born. They were conceived by us and were, thus, born with a disobedient heart.

That reminds me of the little boy who was riding his tricycle furiously around the block over and over again. He just kept going in circles. Finally a policeman stopped and asked him, "Why are you going around and around the block?" The boy said, "Because I'm running away from home. My dad made me do something I didn't want to do." Then the policeman asked, "Why do you keep just going around the block?"

To which the boy responded, "Because my dad said that I'm not allowed to cross the street."

The heart of the human problem is the problem of the human heart. No clever arrangement of bad eggs can make a good omelet. Consequently, we *don't need* to teach our child to disobey. They already know how to do that quite nicely, thank you. To the contrary, they must be taught to obey. We must teach them *not* to lie.

Once one of our children, when very young, began to tell some obvious lies. After further "interrogation," Anne and I realized that he was definitely not telling the truth. We applied enough soap to his mouth to bathe an entire football team. Only after an entire week of a steady diet of soap, and going through God's Word with him, did he finally come clean (no pun intended).

Even Jesus Himself had to be taught obedience—and He didn't even have a sin nature. The Bible says, "Although He was a Son, He learned obedience from the things which He suffered" (Hebrews 5:8). If Jesus Christ Himself, the virgin-born Son of God without a sin nature, had to learn obedience, how much more must our sons and daughters be taught obedience? Every father must take the initiative to rechannel their children's hearts toward doing what God wants them to do.

So, dads, we must teach our children obedience because their hearts are prone to disobey, even in their most erringly innocent moments.

RESPONSIBILITY #2:
DADS, DEFINE OBEDIENCE!
"Children, obey your parents in the Lord, for this is right.
EPHESIANS 6:1

If children are to obey, they must know what is required of them. The boundaries must be clearly defined. Therefore, fathers must teach their children right and wrong, what is acceptable and what is not acceptable.

When Paul says, "Children, obey your parents" (Ephesians 6:1), the word he uses for obey *(hupoacuo)* means literally "to hear under." This Greek word is actually two words which are joined together. *Acuo,* a verb meaning "to hear," is the root of our English word acoustics; which refers to the capacity of hearing. The Greek prefix, *hupo,* meaning "under," is placed before it. So, *hupoacuo* means for children to come under their parents' instruction and listen with the intent of obeying. They must pay attention to what their parents have to say and do it. To hear and not to do is not to hear at all.

Clearly, this presupposes that fathers are teaching their children first. You can't hear what is not being said. If children are to *listen up,* then dads must *speak up.*

Home is to be the university of life. Dad is the president and head professor, mom is on faculty and the head of her department, and, yes, she has tenure! The children form the student body, and the Word of God is the core curriculum. School is always in session, and obedience is what brings a passing grade.

PUTTING IT INTO PRACTICE

Before we move ahead any further, I would like to make several key observations from verse one. Each truth adds a necessary aspect to the total picture of teaching our children obedience.

First, *dads must teach their children the Word of God.* That much is implied by the little phrase "in the Lord." In other words, children are to obey their parents to the extent that what dad is teaching is "in the Lord," or that it squares with the Word of God. Therefore, every father must be a careful student of God's word so that he himself will know how to properly instruct his children.

Secondly, *dads must continually teach their children the Word of God.* The word for "children" *(tekna)* refers to any child living under his or her parent's roof whether they are young or old. This means as soon as the child is old enough to know right from wrong, dads should begin to teach them in the Lord. They should be consistently instructed over and over again throughout the time they are living at home.

Third, *what dads teach their children must be supported by mom.* Paul says that children are to obey their *parents* (plural). Only if dad and mom are teaching the same thing can this be possible. Both parents must speak with one voice. Dad cannot teach one thing and mom teach something else. The two must be operating off the same page of the playbook.

Solomon calls for this same oneness between both parents when he says, "Hear, my son, your *father's* instruction, and do not forsake your *mother's* teaching. Indeed, they are a graceful wreath to your head, and ornaments about your neck" (Proverbs 1:8–9). This implies that the "father's instruction" and "mother's teaching" are one and the same. (What Mom and Dad teach, Solomon says, weave together, or should come together to form one beautiful garland of truth. Two parents, but one garland.)

Sometimes in Proverbs, this parental instruction is referred to simply as the instruction of the father. "Hear, O sons, the instruction of a *father,* and give attention that you may gain understanding" (Proverbs 4:1). But other times, it is the instruction of both Dad and Mom (Proverbs 6:20) as in "My son, observe the commandment of your *father*, and do not forsake the teaching of your *mother*" (Proverbs 6:20). So, whether it's just Dad's instruction, or whether it's both Dad's and Mom's teaching, it is the same signal being sent and the same values being imparted to their children.

Solomon also said, "A wise *son* makes a father glad, but a foolish son is a grief to his *mother*" (Proverbs 10:1). Again, "A wise *son* makes a father glad, but a foolish man despises his *mother*" (Proverbs 15:20). If a wise son gladdens his father and if a foolish son grieves his mother, then Dad and Mom must be teaching the same thing. It's impossible for a wise son to make his father glad, while at the same time grieving his mom, if they're both teaching the same truths.

TIME OUT FOR THE GAME PLAN

Let me suggest something, men. Why don't you sit down with your wife and discuss together what will be your common approach to parenting. What are the common values that you will hold together? What will be the rules of behavior and conduct for your children by which you will run your house? What will be the corresponding punishment when those rules are broken? Get together on this.

One of the greatest experiences that Anne and I ever shared together was to watch a set of video tapes created by John MacArthur and Gary Ezzo entitled, *Parenting With No Regret*. After viewing the videos with some other couples, we worked through a study guide with questions, and shared our answers out loud with other couples. Then, after each session, Anne and I went out for dinner and discussed what we had just learned. In the process, we forged a common game plan for our parenting.

Each of our children at some point growing up has not liked the instruction that they got from Anne during the day while I was at work. In response to what she's told them to do she's heard this response more than once, "But, Dad's the boss…" If they don't like it, they'll appeal to a higher authority with hopes that what I'll say will be different than what Anne said.

As a result, we came to common agreement about what would be acceptable and unacceptable behavior in our home. We formulated a unified approach to our discipline and agreed together what specific punishment would be given for what specific type disobedience. As a result, whether I was with the kids, or whether Anne was with them, we would speak with one voice.

Such a unified front is tremendously important because without it, our children would play one of us against the other in a good cop/bad cop scenario. Now, our children have grown to understand that they can expect the same discipline from Anne as from me. So, when one of us corrects them, there is no need for them to shop around for a better deal.

RESPONSIBILITY #3:
DADS, DEVELOP OBEDIENCE!
Children, obey your parents in the Lord, for this is right.
EPHESIANS 6:1

Dads, after we teach and define obedience, we must reinforce it. This requires creating a home environment where obedience is strongly desired to be pursued by our children. Establishing such a family atmosphere involves both positive and painful reinforcement.

POSITIVE REINFORCEMENT

The most powerful motivation is always positive motivation. How is this achieved?

First, *obedience should be expected.* Obedience is often a self-fulfilled prophecy. Many times if we simply expect our children to obey, they will. The Bible says love "believes all things, hopes all things" (1 Corinthians 13:7). When we believe and hope the best from our children, that has powerful effect upon them. When we say, "I believe that you will do right in this situation," that motivates them to want to prove us right.

Second, *obedience should be praised.* Every child has a deep-seated longing for his or her father's approval. To this day, I still long to receive my father's approval in whatever I do. Although he is seventy-one years old and I have long since left home, his words of affirmation are still a powerful motivation to me. Similarly, our verbal praise for our children when they do right reinforces their obedience, and causes them to obey again in the future.

James Dobson says that we should praise our children seven times for every word of correction. Think about it. If we don't give them a lot of positive reinforcement and only give them correction, they'll grow up thinking that their middle name is "Sit down" or "Be quiet." Our children need heavy doses of our praise.

Third, *obedience should be rewarded.* There are appropriate times to express your approval of exceptional behavior and positive attitude through the bestowing of rewards. Christ offers rewards to us and, in so doing, motivates and encourages our obedience. Jesus says, "Behold, I come quickly and My reward is with Me to give to every man according to his work" (Revelation 22:12). By saying this, He is motivating us to obey Him.

The same approach works at home with our children. Amazingly, my children are motivated to obey when I make it worth their while to complete a task. If I was to offer a reward for every act of obedience, then a reward loses its motivation. But, when strategically offered for exceptional obedience, it becomes a powerful reinforcement. Depending upon the age of your child, you may want, unexpectedly and from time to time, to reward obedience for picking up their room, or for promptly obeying what their mom asked them to do.

PAINFUL REINFORCEMENT

The role of discipline is to teach that there are painful consequences to disobedience. Better that they learn this now while they're home than later in society. Better to learn now the pain associated with disobedience when the issues are relatively small than later when the issues are life threatening like driving fast cars, and disobeying the law when their life is at risk.

Painful reinforcement is the punishment that a father gives to his children for their wrong behavior or bad attitudes. There are various levels of punishments where more serious offenses deserve a more severe punishment. The varying levels of punishments are: (1) verbal rebuke, (2) isolation, (3) loss of privilege, (4) natural consequences, (5) spanking. These subjects will be covered in greater length in chapter 9, titled, "It all Starts at the 'Bottom.'"

At this point though I simply want to establish that we must reinforce obedience with our children through painful punishments—or our instruction will merely become advice, suggestion, or platitude.

For example, when the new school year started this past August, Anne planned a new routine for picking up our three oldest at school in which she told them where they were to be picked up. It was a plan that called for our two seventh grade boys to walk across campus to where their younger sister's third grade class would be waiting.

Well, our junior high boys thought they were "too cool" to be caught dead near the lowly third graders, and their *sister* at that! So, the next day they stayed with their own classmates after school got out rather than go where they were asked to go to be picked up.

On the way home from school, Anne explained again where she wanted them to be picked up and why. The next day when school was out, one of our twins obeyed and walked down to his sister with the third graders for pick up. But our other son—I won't divulge any names to protect the guilty— chose to do his own thing and talk to his friends. Needless to say, Anne was not pleased.

It just so happened that this night was a big high school football game which they were dying to attend. In fact, they were part of the "Chain Gang" that worked the first down marker on the sidelines, something they relished doing each week.

But when Anne explained to me the disobedience of our son, I knew that there needed to be a painful reinforcement. I sure didn't want to, but I had to tell him that he could not go to the game that night, but would have to stay home with his sister, I might add. I hated to make such a call, but it was for his own good.

Men, are you reinforcing obedience with your children? Have you eased up too much in your discipline? Are you letting your children's acts of dis- obedience slide by unpunished? Remember, you must reinforce obedience at home.

RESPONSIBILITY #4:
DADS, DEMONSTRATE OBEDIENCE!
Children, obey your parents in the Lord, for this is right.
EPHESIANS 6:1

Obedience is as much caught as it is taught. Our children will do as we do before they do what we say. I've already mentioned the old saying, "Your actions speak so loudly, I can't hear a word you're saying." That certainly is true in fathering. The obedience that we model deeply impacts our children and influences them to do likewise. Remember, like produces like. We must model the message.

Children naturally emulate their father. Paul understood this when he said to the believers at Corinth, "I do not write these things to shame you, but to admonish you as my beloved children. For if you were to have countless tutors in Christ, yet you would not have many fathers; for in Christ Jesus I became your father through the gospel. I exhort you therefore, be imitators of me" (1 Corinthians 4:14–16). The church in Corinth had many teachers, but only one spiritual father. Only one person had led them to personal faith in Christ and they must follow his example. In other words, the apostle says, "Follow me as I follow Christ."

It's almost scary how much my children imitate me. On Sunday mornings, I leave home at 5:50 A.M. to head to church and have my two shadows at my side—Andrew and James. It's like we're cut out with a cookie cutter. I preach in the same navy suit every Sunday, with a white button-down shirt, black lace-up shoes, and white pocket handkerchief. My only change to "the uniform" is which burgundy striped tie I will have on.

Guess who's dressed just like me? You guessed it, the Bobbsey twins. Navy blazer, white button-down shirt, black lace-up shoes, white pocket stay, and alternating burgundy striped tie. The influence of a dad is real, and it is powerful.

I know that the day will soon come when they will want to establish their own identity, but for right now, I am the strongest role model in their life. While I can, I must capture that opportunity for good and influence them to dress themselves with obedience as they see me doing the same.

Dads, we model for our precious children what obedience looks like. When they see it in us, it leaves a lasting impression upon them and makes them want to live an obedient life, as well.

THE CATCH OF A LIFETIME

I clipped an article from *Readers Digest* several years ago. It's entitled, "The Catch of a Lifetime." I could never read this without being moved to tears.

He was eleven years old and went fishing every time he got to the dock at his family's cabin on an island in the middle of a New Hampshire lake. On the day before the bass season opened, he and his father were fishing early in the evening, catching sunfish and perch with worms. Then he tied on a small silver lure and practiced casting. The lure struck the water and caused colored ripples in the sunset and then silver ripples as the moon rose over the lake.

When his pole doubled over he knew something huge was on the other end. His father watched with admiration as the boy skillfully worked the fish alongside the dock. Finally, he gingerly lifted the exhausted fish from the waters. It was the largest one he had ever seen, but it was a bass. The father and the boy looked at the handsome fish, gills playing back and forth in the moonlight.

The father lit a match and looked at his watch. It was 10:00 P.M., two hours before the bass season opened. He looked at the fish and then at the boy. "You'll have to put it back in the lake, son," he said.

"Dad!" cried the boy.

"There will be other fish," said the father.

"But not as big as this one," he cried as he looked around the lake. No other fishermen or boats were anywhere around in the moonlight. He looked again at his father. Even though no one had seen them nor could anyone ever know what time he caught the fish, the boy could tell by the clarity of his father's voice that the decision was nonnegotiable.

He slowly worked the hook out of the lip of the huge bass and lowered it into the black water. The creature swished his powerful body away and disappeared. The boy suspected that he would never again see such a fish.

That was thirty-four years ago. Today, the boy is a successful architect in New York City. His father's cabin is still there on the island in the middle of the lake. He takes his own son and daughters fishing from the very same dock from which his father took him fishing.

The boy was right. He has never again caught such a magnificent fish as the one he landed that night long ago, but he does see that same fish again and again every time he comes up with a question of ethics in his business. For as his father taught him, ethics are simple matters of right and wrong. It's only the practice of ethics that is difficult.

Do we do what is right when no one is looking? Do we refuse to cut corners to get the design in on time? Do we refuse to trade stocks based on information we weren't supposed to have? We would if we were taught to put the fish back when we were a little child.[2]

Men, *that's* preparing a will before it's too late.

CHAPTER 6

DON'T LEAVE HOME WITHOUT IT!

A Legacy of Respect

WHEN I WAS A BOY OF FOURTEEN, MY FATHER WAS SO IGNORANT
I COULD HARDLY STAND TO HAVE THE OLD MAN AROUND.
BUT WHEN I GOT TO BE TWENTY-ONE, I WAS ASTONISHED AT HOW MUCH
THE OLD MAN HAD LEARNED.
—*Mark Twain*

We try to make every birthday at our house a special event. But I must admit that James's and Andrew's tenth birthday "took the cake."

After saving up enough frequent flier miles, I flew the three of us to see a Chicago Bull's basketball game featuring the Human Highlight Film himself, Michael Jordan. You know, just a little male bonding. It was an unforgettable experience as we witnessed Jordan pour in fifty-two points. However, it was the trip to Chicago that proved to be the most memorable.

When the big day came for us to leave, our entire family came to the airport to see us off. This was history in the making at the Lawson house! As we pulled up at the curbside, the porter checked our baggage and I told Anne and the kids to head on to the gate. I would park the car and meet them there.

In a few minutes, I caught up with Anne and the kids at our departure gate. As people were ready to board the plane, Anne said, "You'd better give me my car keys before you fly to Chicago with them in your pocket."

Of course, she was right. It would be just like me to forget to give her the keys back and leave her stranded at the airport. So, I began to frisk myself for the keys. I found my billfold and cash, but I couldn't find the car keys anywhere. "My keys!" I panicked, "Where are my keys?"

Then all of a sudden, it hit me.

As the loud speaker called for our flight to board, I took off running down the corridor as fast as I could. I flew down the escalator, sprinted through the lobby, and rushed out to the curbside where I discovered it was still there. Just as I had left it. There it was, still parked at curbside—our Suburban!

The engine was still *running*. All four doors were *wide open*. The windshield wipers were still *going*. The lights were still *on*. And the back tailgate was *still down*.

I had completely *forgotten* to park our car.

You know what? I was so excited about flying to Chicago with my boys that I left the car running in the loading zone. I went absolutely brain dead and forgot to park it. I just left it there. Running.

After I parked the Suburban, I dashed back to the gate where our flight had already boarded. Anne, somewhat exasperated, said, "Where have you been?"

I said, "Well, you're not going to believe this, but I *forgot* to park the car."

With a bewildered look on her face, she exclaimed, "I *can't believe* that I'm entrusting my two firstborn sons to you to take to Chicago…and you can't even remember to park the car in Little Rock!"

Men, I hope you've never been *that* forgetful and left home with your car running at the airport. We all can become so preoccupied and focused that we neglect the most basic responsibilities as it relates to raising and caring for our children. But worse than forgetting to park our car at the airport is neglecting to pass down the core values that will leave a legacy of godliness.

In this chapter, we come to the fourth core value that we must build into our children—*respect!* Don't let them leave home without it.

If there was one thing I was taught growing up, it was to respect my parents. That was drilled into me from the beginning of my childhood. And, you know, respecting one's parents wasn't uncommon in those days. I was taught to say "Yes, sir" and "No, ma'am" every time my parents spoke to me. If I've said, "Yes, sir" once, I've said it a million times. Never, "Huh?", nor, "Un ahh." To this day, if anyone near my age or older speaks to me, I say, "Yes, sir," "Yes, ma'am."

My father taught me to shake hands with adults, to look them in the eye, and to squeeze their hand harder than they squeezed mine. No limp wristed, cold-fish handshakes were allowed. No mumbled "Yes, sir" was acceptable. My parents taught me to be quiet when they were talking, and I never talked back to them. The thought never entered my mind. I never questioned my parents. I never argued with them. I never raised my voice to them.

Unfortunately, such respect seems to be a fading page of ancient history. Gone the way of the flattop. As I've taught my children these same values, they are often ostracized because they cut against the grain of where the majority of children are today. To talk about respect in this day and time is to be radically countercultural. In its place, we have a generation of young people in which dishonor and disrespect are in vogue. Television sitcoms portray parents as incompetent and encourage young people to be irreverent towards all authority figures.

Instead of giving respect, young people now demand it!

I believe that all this goes back to the lack of fear of God in our society. Because we have lost our reverence for God, we have declared "open season" on all authority figures.

Dads, if this trend is to change, it can only be reversed at home. We are the last hope for restoration of real family values as touted by many politicians. We must instill respect in our children, and it must begin at an early age. Honoring parents is an indispensable core value that must be taught in every home.

Respect...don't let them leave home without it!

Let's discover now how to develop respect in the hearts of our children. Just as we must teach our children obedience (Ephesians 6:1), so we must teach them respect (verses 2–3).

TRUTH #1:
DADS, DEFINE RESPECT!

Honor your father and mother; (which is the first
commandment with a promise), that it may be well
with you, and that you may live long on the earth.
EPHESIANS 6:2–3

We must first understand what the word "honor" really means. According to *Webster's Dictionary,* honor means "high public esteem, fame, glory, to earn a position of honor." To honor one's parents is to give them deep respect and to show them the appreciation, esteem, and high regard that is due them.

In the original Hebrew language, honor *(kabod)* comes from a root that means "to be heavy." A great person was considered to be "heavy" because his wealth was measured in terms of gold, silver, and other valuable possessions. The wealthier a person was, the heavier they were in terms of personal assets. Such a person commanded great respect in the community because of their vast net worth. Great weight was given to them and to whatever they said.

To honor one's parents means to recognize their great value and to weigh them down with respect and admiration. Who they are and what they say are considered to be very weighty and important. In showing them respect, a child is saying to his or her parents, "I place upon you great worth and value."

When children honor their parents, they act politely and obediently toward them, while speaking kindly to and about them. By action and attitude, a child's respect recognizes that they are the persons whom God has sovereignly placed over their lives to raise and care for them. Honoring one's parents requires submission to their authority, obedience to their requests, teachableness toward their instruction, and thankfulness toward their goodness.

What constitutes honoring one's parents? What does respect look like? What does it sound like?

Respect comes in many different forms.

First, it involves a *respectful attitude.* It begins as an attitude in the heart of our children that causes them to regard us with love and devotion. To honor one's parents is to possess a general outlook of esteem, reverence, and deference. No matter what the child's actions express, respect is first and foremost a matter of the heart.

A little girl was being disciplined by her father because of her selfish actions. As a result, she was told to sit in the corner. After fifteen minutes of isolation, her dad asked her if she had learned her lesson. Stubbornly, the little girl said, "I may be sitting down on the outside, but I'm standing up on the inside."

That describes a lot of children—outwardly obedient, but inwardly unyielding. Respect begins with the heart of a child being compliant toward his or her parents. The attitude must be right before anything else can be right.

Second, it includes *respectful words.* Our children should address us with words that are respectful and reflect our high position assigned by God. This should include saying, "Yes, sir," "No, ma'am," "Thank you," and "Please." Respect is always polite and shows regard for our God-given authority in the Lord. They should never call us by our first name. Likewise, a child should never call us into question, or talk back in a short or curt fashion. If they disagree with something, an appeal may be made, but only in a way that shows deference and reverence.

There has been much training on our part to teach our children to do this. Having done this now with four children, I am so well trained myself that sometimes I find myself correcting other children out of habit.

Third, it involves a *respectful tone of voice*. There is a tone of voice that is acceptable for a child to a parent and one that is unacceptable. A sarcastic tone is simply disrespect in disguise. So also is mimicking, insincerity, and halfhearted answers. Dads, never allow pouting or whining from your children, nor shouting or angry outbursts toward you or your wife. Such tones of voice are unquestionably unacceptable.

Fourth, it includes a *respectful facial expression*. Our children's faces are powerful mediums of communication. With their countenance, they should also express the honor due their parents. By their facial expression, they can communicate disrespect through a mean frown, or a resistant scowl. Eye contact is a part of this also. Our children should look us in the eye when spoken to. To ignore us and look away when we speak to them is disrespect.

Fifth, it involves a *respectful body posture*. When spoken to, children should sit up straight or stand alert. This shows that they are paying attention and what you are saying is important. Body posture reflects attitude. Being laid back or slumped over communicates apathy and indifference, as does putting their hands on their hips in a condescending fashion.

I was recently made aware of a family that was visiting in another home. Their little boy, age five, had to be corrected by the other mother, something his own parents refused to do. Amazingly, this young tot walked over and put his hand over the woman's mouth and said for all to hear, "Be quiet." Even more amazing, his father did nothing to correct such defiance. This ought not to be.

Sixth, it includes *respectful manners*. Respect is communicated by showing common manners, such as rising when their mother or another adult enters the room, opening the door for them, pulling out a lady's chair at the dinner table, or allowing an adult to walk through the door first. Our children must also be taught not to interrupt when we are speaking, but to wait until the appropriate time to speak. Manners are the polish that makes respect attractive.

The other day, Anne and the children were taking a guest of ours to church. John was already in the car waiting. But as Anne and this lady approached the car, he began to scramble out of the car. Anne reprimanded him, telling him to stay in the car. As he protested, Anne thought she would have to render discipline. Finally he said, "I wanted to open Miss Jo's door for her."

John wanted to do this because he had seen his older brothers doing it, who had seen their dad do it. This is the way good training ought to be passed down.

Seventh, it involves *respectful appearance.* Now this may sound legalistic, but I think children ought to dress a certain way when they are around their parents. For example, when they come to the dinner table, children ought to look more presentable than an unmade bed. Call me old fashioned, but boys ought to have a shirt on, as well as shoes. If McDonald's won't serve you barefooted, then neither should we. After mom has worked hard to prepare a meal, it shows her respect and says that she is special and appreciated. Likewise, inappropriate dress in public by our children sends a subtle signal that says, "I don't want to fit in with Mom and Dad."

Eighth, it includes *respectful actions.* Honoring parents requires obedience from the heart. Children should obey with a submissive attitude the first time addressed, and to do so with a gentle and quiet spirit. They must not meet our requests with resistance, arguing, or defiance, but with first-time obedience. Delayed obedience is no obedience.

This is the kind of respect that we must cultivate in our children. Now, I admit, showing honor like this is just not the norm. It sounds like a rerun of Ozzie and Harriet. But it must, I believe, be taught and instilled at home, or it will never happen. It requires our constant reinforcement if it is to become real in our homes.

Dads, do you see what respect looks like? What we are talking about here encompasses the whole of a child's life from attitudes, to words, to tone of voice, to countenance, to gestures, to manners, to appearance, and finally to their actions. It's the total package—a lifestyle.

TRUTH #2:
DADS, DEMAND RESPECT!
Honor your father and mother (which is the first
commandment with a promise) that it may be well
with you, and that you may live long upon the earth.
EPHESIANS 6:2–3

Showing respect for one's parents is a virtue commanded by God. It's non-negotiable, called for in His Word, something that every father must teach his children to do.

These two verses are a direct quote from Exodus 20:12, where God gave the Ten Commandments to His people. These timeless absolutes would form the foundation for Israel as a nation, by teaching them how to relate to God and to live with one another.

This commandment, Paul says, is the "first commandment with a promise." Although it is listed fifth, it is the first that carried a specific promise of special blessing attached to it. That's because it is so strategically important in relationship to the other Ten Commandments. The first four commandments govern our relationship to God (Exodus 20:1–11), while the last six commandments govern our relationship toward others (Exodus 20:12–20). The fifth commandment stands uniquely between these two parts and, as such, is the bridge between loving God and loving others. Honoring parents should be the direct and immediate result of our faith in God. In other words, obeying the first four commandments should show itself to be real by obeying the fifth commandment.

God said, "He who strikes a man so that he dies shall surely be put to death" (Exodus 21:12). Clearly, the Bible teaches capital punishment in the case of deliberate, premeditated murder. If you take someone's life, then your life ought to be taken by the government. This judicial retribution is required because of the value which God assigns to human life created in His image (Genesis 1:26–27; 9:6).

But what is number two on the list of offenses worthy of capital punishment? The answer might be surprising, but not when we consider how important it is to God. What is this serious sin? It is showing disrespect toward one's parents.

God says, "And he who strikes his father or mother shall surely be put to death… And he who curses his father or his mother shall surely be put to death." (Exodus 21:15, 17). Now, that's pretty strong medicine, isn't it? In Old Testament times, children who physically hit their parents, or who were disrespectful to them, were to be immediately stoned to death. If we were still under the Old Covenant today, this would wipe out an entire generation. Talk about a generation gap!

If you honored your parents, you would live long because you would escape the death penalty. Longevity of life is still true today for obeying this commandment, but in a different way. True, we no longer are under the Mosaic Law which assigns the death penalty for dishonoring one's parents. But if our children will honor us when we say, "Don't play in the street," they will most assuredly live longer. If they will honor us when we say, "Don't play with fire," or "Don't play with guns," they will live longer. If they will honor us when we say, "Buckle your seat belt" or "Don't take drugs," they will live longer. So, even today, this promise has meaning.

At the same time, children honoring parents not only adds years to their life ("that you may live long on the earth"), but also it adds life to their years ("that it may be well with you"). If our children will honor us, they will position themselves to receive the fullness of God's goodness. When my children show respect for me, I am more likely to go the extra mile to lavish my goodness upon them than when they are disrespectful. At the same time, we dads must require the respect of our children towards their mothers. This is something that we reinforce for our wives. Moms need all the help they can get.

Although we are no longer under the Law today, the Old Covenant reveals the great importance that God attaches to children honoring their parents. This is a timeless truth, regardless of the era in which we live.

In Leviticus 19:1, God said, "You shall be holy for I, the Lord, am holy." In so doing, God was saying, "I want you to be just like Me in your character and life." Now, notice the first requirement mentioned if we are to be holy like He is holy. "Every child shall reverence his own mother and father" (verse 2). Respect for parents was a leading indicator of personal holiness.

Dads, if God places such a high importance upon children honoring their parents, then so must we. If our homes are to be holy, then requiring respect from our children must be a priority.

TRUTH #3:
DADS, DEVELOP RESPECT!

*Honor your father and mother (which is the first
commandment with a promise) that it may be well
with you, and that you may live long upon the earth.*

EPHESIANS 6:2–3

Respect must be cultivated within the heart of a child. So, how can we do this? Let me offer some practical steps to take.

First, *teach respect for God.* Remember, the first four commandments deal with how we are to relate to God. The fifth commandment then calls us to honor our parents. This strategic placement in the Ten Commandments suggests that honoring parents is the direct result of loving God. If our children are taught to reverence God (Exodus 20:1–11), then respect for us will follow naturally (Exodus 20:12).

Solomon, the wisest man who ever lived, wrote, "The fear of the Lord is the beginning of knowledge; fools despise wisdom and instruction. Hear, my son, your father's instruction, and do not forsake your mother's teaching" (Proverbs 1:7–8). In other words, honoring God leads to honoring one's parents. The two go hand-in-hand.

First Peter 2:17 says, "Honor all men; love the brotherhood, fear God, honor the king." Fearing God leads to honoring all other people and authority figures. Certainly, included in this is honoring one's parents. It's a package deal.

Dads, do yourself a favor and teach your children to have a high view of God. The more our children respect God, the more they will respect us.

Second, *explain God's chain of commands.* We should teach our children that God has ordained the "office" of father, and that He has placed us over their lives. Just as God is over us, so we are over our children. It is God's design to lead and love our children through us. They must understand that showing disrespect toward us is showing disrespect toward the One who placed us over them. Our special responsibility should earn special respect.

Also, parents should explain to their children that, though they are fallible, they are to be considered worthy of honor. Honoring parents is a matter of a child living by faith, regardless of their parent's performance, behavior, or dysfunction. Every child must trust that God in His infinite wisdom will use his or her parents, limited and finite as they are, to help shape his life into what God wants it to be.

Third, *teach the basics again and again.* Repetition is a great teacher. In fathering, we must teach the basics of showing respect day after day. We must teach what is required in showing respect in all its many forms—attitude, voice tone, facial expression, body posture, manners, appearance, and actions. But it must be taught over and over.

I am constantly having to remind my children to say, "Yes, Ma'am" to their mother, and "Thank you" to me. But at least I am having to do it with less frequency, not more. It must be reinforced again and again.

Since the day they were housebroken, we have taught our children to go to the bathroom and brush their teeth every night before going to bed. I sound like a broken record, but I still have to remind them over and over and over again. Our twins are twelve years old, yet I still have to tell them, "Guys, every night until the Lord comes back, you will go to the bathroom and brush your teeth before you go to bed." If I have to remind them of such basic activities, how much more must we remind our child to show honor and respect towards us.

TRUTH #4:

DADS, DEMONSTRATE RESPECT!

Honor your father and mother (which is the first
commandment with a promise) that it may be well
with you, and that you may live long upon the earth.

EPHESIANS 6:2–3

Dads, how we show respect toward authority figures in our lives has a profound effect upon our sons and daughters. As we model respect for God, this has a powerful and positive effect upon our children. Conversely, our disrespect encourages disrespect in the lives of our children.

A few years ago, I was attending a junior high basketball game where a well-known Christian leader was watching his son play. During the course of the game, the referee made a questionable call against his boy and you would have thought that someone had wounded this man with a shotgun. He collapsed to his knees, and stomped around courtside like an angry bull. Anger toward the referee spewed from his mouth creating quite an ugly scene.

Finally, the school administrator had no choice but to speak to this deranged dad. What a sad scene it was to watch this grown man, a so-called spiritual leader, acting more like a spoiled brat than a man of God. Now, I happen to know that this man was also having difficulty with his son's behavior in school. I think he comes by it naturally.

Dads, we must conduct ourselves in a way that will make it easy for our children to honor us. While respect is required, it must also be earned. When we walk in the power of the Spirit and exemplify Christlikeness, we make it the old-fashioned way—we *earn* it! But when our walk fails to match our talk we make it very difficult for our children to do what God is calling them to do—that is, to honor us.

LITTLE EYES ARE WATCHING

Along this line, let me share an incident from my own life recently that illustrates how important it is to model respect for our children. As a family, we were driving from Mobile, Alabama to the Smoky Mountains, when we approached Greenville, South Carolina. It was late at night and very dark. Suddenly, as we entered the city, the four-lane highway became a busy thoroughfare with traffic lights and bumper to bumper traffic. As I was driving, a large 18-wheel truck pulled into our lane and completely blocked my vision of the upcoming traffic light.

At that exact moment, it turned yellow and then red as I went through the intersection. Unfortunately, the next thing I saw was the flashing blue lights of a state trooper in my rearview mirror.

As I pulled over and got out of my car, two options were before me. Either blow up in anger, or calmly explain my predicament. I chose the later route. First, I told the officer that I believed that he was placed in authority over my life for my good, appreciated his service, and would accept whatever he chose to do. Then, I appealed to him to reconsider giving me a ticket because what happened to me was out of my control.

Guess what? After writing a ticket, he tore it up!

Now if I had gotten angry at him, I can assure you that would have never happened. But I chose to honor him, and it worked for my good.

When I got back in the car, all four of our kids were bug-eyed. This was high drama for our normally squeaky-clean lives. Realizing that this was a great teaching opportunity with my children, I explained that the police officer chose not to give me the ticket. The reason why, I explained, was because I showed him respect. Not in a manipulative way, but in a sincere fashion. Then I urged them to always show respect to those in authority over them. Maybe not immediately as in this case, but somehow, somewhere, sometime, I told them, it would come back to bless them. And it will.

The point here, men, is we must model respect. Let me ask you: how do you talk about your boss at home? Remember, little ears are listening. How do you speak about the President of the United States? How do you talk about the governor or other politicians? How do you reference the pastor at the dinner table after church? How do you talk about your own parents, or your in-laws? How you show respect will leave a lasting impression on your children. Don't just teach it—model it!

Let me say it again, God highly values children honoring their parents. When our children honor us, God will honor them. I don't know what you've been thinking while you've been reading this chapter. But I've got to tell you, these are timeless truths, rooted and grounded in the Word of God, that must be implemented in the lives of our children. We've got to return to teaching our children to respect us and other authority figures in their lives, and if they will, God promises to bless them greatly.

In closing, let me share one such example from the life of our family. A couple of years ago, I bought a picture of the eighteenth green at Augusta National, framed it, and hung it over James's bed. We have it, not only because Augusta National is a beautiful golf course, but because it's a constant reminder to us of a special lesson in learning to show respect.

When my twin sons, James and Andrew, were five years old, I took them to Augusta, Georgia, to the Masters Invitational Golf Tournament. We went to three practice rounds at Augusta, and the boys got everyone's autograph.

I believe that James and Andrew have a spiritual gift of getting autographs. They had gotten so many autographs that the only question in their minds as we drove to the tournament the last day was, "Would they get someone's autograph a *second* time?" They already had everyone's autograph once. But, would they get a second round of autographs? Andrew said yes, James said no.

As we walked onto the course, we walked first to the large putting green by the clubhouse at Augusta National. There were several hundred people standing around the green, watching the pros practice putting.

Tim Simpson, who had just won on the PGA tour the week before, was leaving the putting green and heading to the number one tee box. Andrew went up to him and got his autograph a second time.

Standing right next to Andrew was James, dressed exactly like Andrew, from the top of his head to the bottom of his feet. It was painfully obvious that they were twins. What else could Tim Simpson do but say to Andrew's look alike, "Would you like my autograph too?"

James immediately and rather rudely responded, "No!"

That particular day was not a good attitude day for James. When he said no, he did so with a disrespectful tone in front of many people. In fact, it came across as a put-down. No one in the long history of the Masters had ever turned down an autograph. But James did. As everyone laughed, Simpson's face just turned beet red, and so did mine.

I took James aside and got down on one knee. Eye to eye and face to face, I said to him, "Buddy, you were disrespectful to that man. What's worse, I happen to know he's a Christian brother." Although he was only five, I said, "James, if God gives you the opportunity, I think you need to ask Mr. Simpson for his forgiveness. He was trying to be nice to you and you were very disrespectful."

The rest of the time at the Masters, we tried to catch up with Tim Simpson to make the offense right. But we could never catch him at the right moment. When it came time for us to leave, this issue was still unresolved. As we were walking past the putting green toward the parking lot to drive back home, I looked up and guess who was right before us. Tim Simpson.

"James, here's your chance." He ran over to him and—bless James's heart, I was so proud of him—he stood right in front of this famous golfer, looked up and said, "Mr. Simpson, will you forgive me? I was disrespectful to you earlier today."

James was about knee-high to a grasshopper at the time. Tim Simpson, gracious man that he is, got down on one knee and said, "I remember what you're talking about, and, of course, I forgive you. I've never had a fan come up to me and apologize about anything." Tim gave him a big hug and a smile.

As James and I were walking away, I knew that this was one of those teachable moments in life. So I stopped and said, "James, I'm very proud of you. What you have done is right. I don't know *how*, I don't know *when*, and

I don't know *where,* but God is going to honor you for doing the right thing."

As we began walking toward the parking lot, we passed the eighteenth green. At that exact moment, a large crowd began to move from the green toward the famed Augusta Clubhouse. I honestly thought the President of the United States must be there with an entourage so large. There were television cameras recording, boom mics extended, and security guards clearing a path for whoever this celebrity was. *Whoever* was in there was obviously important. So I walked around to see who it was.

It was none other than Jack Nicklaus, the greatest golfer of all time. James and Andrew had been talking for months about getting his autograph. And that was the *only* autograph they didn't have. I said, "Look, James, there's Jack Nicklaus."

"Dad, I'm gonna go get his autograph."

I said, "Buddy, you can't. There's too many people in there."

But before I could say anything else, James bolted right into the middle of that swarm of people. He wormed his way through that moving mass of arms and legs, and before I knew it he was out of sight. He was going to be trampled to death and my first thought was, "Anne is going to kill me for sure."

Clutching Andrew's hand, I ran around to the other side of the crowd to try to find James. After what seemed an eternity, I got to the other side. You won't believe what I saw. A Pinkerton security guard had picked James up and was walking backwards with him hoisted up, in front of Jack Nicklaus's face. James was holding a piece of paper with two hands while Jack Nicklaus was signing his autograph.

The security guard finally put James down, and he came running out of that pack, waving his prized piece of paper over his head, yelling, "Daddy, Daddy, Daddy, I got his autograph! I got his autograph!"

Suddenly I remembered what I had just shared with him, "Son, God is going to honor you for doing the right thing. Sometime, somewhere, someplace, somehow, God is going to honor you."

And He did.

CHAPTER 7

STRONG HANDS, TENDER HEARTS

A Legacy of Gentleness

RULES WITHOUT RELATIONSHIP LEADS TO REBELLION.

—*Howard Hendricks*

When Anne and I were expecting our third child, all the older women in our church kept telling me, "We sure are praying this will be a girl. You sure need a little girl. It will help round you out!"

A *girl?*

What would I do with a girl?

I knew how to relate to boys. You buy a football and play catch with them. You go to baseball games together. You wrestle with one another on the floor. You know, *guy* things.

But a girl? Just the mere thought scared me to death. And these same women kept saying, "Oh, a little girl will have you wrapped around her little finger. Just you wait and see." What were they talking about?

Well, God knew exactly what I needed. He knew that I *did* need a sweet little girl. Someone to make me more patient and understanding, more sensitive and gentle, more compassionate and caring. Bringing a little girl into my life was one of God's effective tools to bring out qualities in my life that needed maturing. Now, don't get me wrong, I haven't become Mr. Touchy-Feely, but you should have seen me before.

I'll never forget when Grace Anne was born, one of the doctors in our church said to me, "One of the great things about having a girl is that she is never too old to sit in your lap and hug your neck."

You know, he was right. When I come home at the end of the day, the first one—and sometimes the *only* one—to run out the front door to greet me with a hug is Grace Anne. When I travel out of town, she's the one that says, "Daddy, please don't go! How soon will you be back?" My boys actually want me to go so I'll bring them a present.

I'm not there completely, but God is in the process of giving me a more tender heart to go with my strong hands. I hate to admit it, but those older ladies were right. I did need a little girl. And God is using her to make me a "kinder, gentler" man.

Men, we all need to have a gentle side to us. One aspect of the fruit of the Spirit is gentleness (Galatians 5:23). Every godly father will be marked by gentleness—no exceptions. Some men are absolute bears at home, growling at everything that moves. But a godly man is not easily irritated, nor harsh. In short, we need to be Christlike, and that means, among other things, having a gentle spirit. Jesus said of Himself, "For I am gentle and humble in heart; and you shall find rest for your souls" (Matthew 11:29).

What does gentleness mean? What does it look like?

Simply put, gentleness is tenderness. It is a sensitive heart that causes every father to deal with his children in a calm and controlled manner. Our strength must be tempered by sensitivity, our toughness with tenderness.

In this chapter, we will look at how we, as dads, must show gentleness toward our children. I want to zero in on some practical ways in which we can avoid, as Paul says, provoking our children to anger. Here's how to leave a legacy of gentleness and what it'll take on our part... *strong hands and tender hearts.*

CHALLENGE #1:
DADS, BE PATIENT!
Fathers, do not provoke your children to anger.
EPHESIANS 6:4A

Gentle fathers are, first of all, patient. Patience has been defined as letting your motor idle when you feel like stripping the gears. We need that, because when we are impatient, we provoke our children to anger—even when we are trying to serve God and help them.

I heard about one preacher recently who became so absorbed in his sermon preparation that he was difficult to live with. His daughter said, "Dad, can we buy the house next door?"

"Why would you want to move next door?" he asked.

"No, no," his daughter replied. "We wouldn't move next door. *You* would move next door when you're working on a sermon."

Out of the mouths of babes.

Why would the apostle Paul issue a caution to every father, "And fathers, do not provoke your children to anger" (Ephesians 6:4a)? Because we men have a natural tendency to be too demanding and domineering. We can be too impatient and overbearing. That kind of operating style may work with your competitors at work, but it won't fly at home. Consequently, the apostle needed to speak to every father in an attempt to divert us from abusing our God-given authority over our children.

KEEP YOUR COOL!

Let me tell you how not to do it. Anne, our four children, and I had been out of town on a family trip and after a full day cooped up together in the car, our kids began to get restless and, shall we say, hyperactive. Which, interpreted, means a full scale civil war was breaking out in the back seats.

I looked up in the rearview mirror and told everyone to settle down. Unfortunately, that had no effect whatsoever on the group dynamic. It only created a temporary truce, long enough to allow everyone to reload and refire.

In a matter of moments, our kids were at it again. Wrestling. Jabbing. Poking. Arguing. Pretty soon, I heard cries, "Dad, he hit me." And, "Dad, she's on my side." And, "Stop it...Daddy, tell him to stop it!"

Once more, I raised my voice, "Settle down."

Again, to no avail.

By this point, smoke was spewing out of my ears. Wheeling around to the back seat, I said something profoundly spiritual, like, "If you don't knock it off, I'm going to pull this car over, and then nobody's going to be happy." If I couldn't be happy, I was bound and determined that no one else would be either.

After a few moments of silence, the rumble started back up again. Our once normal kids were at it again. Whining. Screaming. Complaining. Tattling. And, of all things—now get this—giggling.

That was it. I'd *had* it.

I stomped on the brakes and swerved our car over to the side of the busy interstate highway. Amazingly, the car got so quiet you could hear the grass growing outside.

I threw open my door and stormed around to the other side of the Suburban, jerked open the side door, and pronounced the death penalty on my two oldest sons. I fished them out of the rear seat and lined them up outside the car in single file as if they were facing a firing squad.

Mind you, this was during five o'clock rush-hour traffic on an eight lane interstate, only one exit away from our church on the same highway. Half the town was witnessing this execution.

I was so upset, I could have exploded! I began to read them their last rites when James, eight years old at the time, did something completely unfair. He began to *cry*.

All of a sudden, it hit me like a 2x4 across the forehead. Here I was, intimidating my poor kids to death, upset because they were out of control. *I* was the one out of control. Granted, they deserved to be reprimanded, even punished. But not marched off to a death camp.

Like I said, here's how *not* to do it.

I had to back off immediately and change my tune, along with asking for their forgiveness. I had completely blown it and was attempting to carry out my fathering, not in the Spirit, but in the flesh. I was so right, I was wrong.

Can you identify with that? I hope not, but if you're honest with yourself, you probably have blown it with your children at some time or another. Probably more than once. But in the power of the Holy Spirit, there is patience (Galatians 5:22).

CHALLENGE #2:
DADS, BE PRUDENT!
Fathers, do not provoke your children to anger.
EPHESIANS 6:4A

We must treat our children fairly. Few things can aggravate them more and cause them to lose heart like uneven treatment at home. This means, as we carry out discipline, the punishment we assign must fit the crime.

When God said, "Life for life, eye for eye, tooth for tooth, hand for hand, foot for foot, burn for burn, wound for wound, bruise for bruise" (Exodus 21:23–25), He was calling for justice. Never an eye for a tooth, nor a hand for a foot, nor a burn for a wound. That would be injustice. But, with fairness and equity, an eye for an eye, a tooth for a tooth. That's where the punishment fits the crime.

Men, we must be careful not to overreact. We exasperate our children when we require the death penalty for every small offense. Don't shoot a mosquito with a canon. Overkill does just that—it kills. One punishment does not fit all crimes. Some offenses simply require verbal reproof, others require isolation, others require natural consequences, others require a withholding of privileges, while still others require physical spanking. We will discuss at greater length in the next chapter when to administer what discipline. But at this point, suffice to say, one size does not fit all. Punishment that is too harsh leads to anger and resentment.

On the other hand, a failure to apply any discipline provokes our children to anger. Deep down inside, they want to know where the boundaries are. They want to know that they are loved, and discipline, when properly applied, proves a parent's love. Let's face it, some children act up just to get their father's attention. "Discipline me, just don't ignore me," is the silent cry of their heart. Sometimes a rebellious child is simply longing for his parent's attention, and a failure to discipline only fuels that anger even more.

Dads, here is the point. Don't be too harsh, don't be too soft. Just be fair. Going to either extreme will lead to resentment by your child, whether expressed by active rebellion or passive indifference. Be balanced in the handling of your discipline. The Bible says, "A false balance is an abomination to the Lord, but a just weight is His delight" (Proverbs 11:1, NKJV). Men, measure your discipline fairly, and listen to your wife as you do. She will be a tempering influence in your life.

CHALLENGE #3:
DADS, BE PREDICTABLE!
Fathers, do not provoke your children to anger.
EPHESIANS 6:4A

Another way that we can cause resentment in our children is when we are inconsistent in our discipline. On one day, we may be too strict, the next day too soft, and our kids never know what to expect from us. One time, they are punished severely for doing a wrong, but then the next time, there's no punishment at all. It's like rearranging the furniture on Helen Keller. They never know what they'll run into next, and that leads to frustration.

For example, there was a behavioral test that a man named Pavlov performed on some dogs. He put a dog in a cage, rang a bell, and a small door then opened with food behind the door. Again and again, this was done. Soon, whenever the bell would ring, the dog would begin to salivate and drool, anticipating the food.

But then, unknown to the dog, Pavlov set up a water hose behind the door. The bell rang, the dog smacked his lips, the door opened, but this time he got a blast of water right in the nose. This threw the dog for a loop.

Pavlov then began to rotate what was behind the door. Sometimes food, sometimes water. When he expected food, he would get a hard blast of water in the face. Whenever the bell would ring, the dog would not come running. No matter how hungry the dog was, when the bell rang, the dog began to shake and tremble. The uncertainty of what was coming—food or a blast of water—drove the dog to a nervous breakdown.

Dads, we can do that to our kids. One day, we're committed to faithful, loving discipline, but the next day we're too tired, or too preoccupied, to get involved. No wonder, when you hit the front door at the end of the day, your kids start to shake and tremble. They don't know who just came home— Jeckle or Hyde. The uncertainty of it can drive them to anger and bitterness. Stop right now and ask yourself, "Am I consistent in my discipline? Do I need to be more faithful? Do I need to change?"

CHALLENGE #4:
DADS, BE PRACTICAL!
Fathers, do not provoke your children to anger.
EPHESIANS 6:4A

Fathers can provoke their children to anger by showing partiality, favoring one child over the other. We must make every effort to be impartial in how we give our time, attention, and compliments. If we favor one child over another, it can lead to bitterness with the others. There are various ways that we do this.

One, we can show favoritism according to our children's *interests*. As men, we have our own preferences and tastes in sports, recreation, and hobbies. When our children share in those interests, it makes it easy to "connect" with them. But sometimes, a child will have different interests and pursue activities in other areas. We must be careful not to favor the children who share our passions, and neglect our children who have different interests. Allow God to be as original in their life as He was in ours.

Two, we can show favoritism according to our children's *gender*. It's been interesting to me to observe to which fathers God gives boys, and to whom He gives girls, and in what order. Sometimes hardheaded dads like me need a little girl to sweeten us up and make us more relational. God knows what He's doing. Let us be careful not to gravitate toward one gender at home and miss some lessons that God desires to teach us.

Three, we can show favoritism according to our children's *abilities*. Unfortunately, it's often easy to get along with the child that excels most successfully in a given area, while neglecting the less gifted child.

A father should never say something like, "Why can't you make good grades like your sister?" Nor, "Why can't you play shortstop like your brother?" Each child should be measured by how they perform their own God-given ability. They should rise or fall on their own merit, not by how they compare with a sibling. Such comparisons can only lead to resentment toward both dad and the "perfect" sibling.

Four, we can show favoritism according to our children's *age*. The natural tendency is for dads to become emotionally bonded with a firstborn child. But when our career takes off and other children come, we no longer have time for the younger children. Or, it could be just the opposite. When you first got married, you were under the time crunch of medical school or in law school and had no discretionary time to give your firstborn. But now, you dote all over your younger children because you have more time. If this favoritism continues, you will most likely breed anger in the neglected child.

CHALLENGE #5:
DADS, BE PRESENT!

Fathers, do not provoke your children to anger.
EPHESIANS 6:4A

Children feel cheated when dad is never home. If this absence runs long enough, anger is sure to brew in the hearts of our children who feel neglected because dad was never around. They become jealous of whatever it is that takes him away. Absentee dads usually have angry sons and daughters.

A recent Christian magazine article revealed the inside struggles of Curt and Chuck Swindoll, Jr., the sons of the famous Dr. Chuck Swindoll, and what it was like to grow up with a super-preacher dad. In this telling interview, the question was asked, "Did you ever feel that you were being let down by a father who was too busy to spend time with you?"

The younger of the two sons, Chuck Jr., answered with transparency and honesty. Let his reply serve as a warning to every workaholic dad. He said, "I felt an increasing amount of bitterness. I felt like I wasn't important enough for dad to spend time with me. Looking back, I feel like he often chose his work rather than me. It made me angry. I didn't want to be around him."

Looking back on his years, Dr. Swindoll's own commentary is revealing, "I say with great sadness today that I wish I had changed more. I regret that I did not make some major changes so I could spend more time with them."

Men, let us heed this warning…before it's too late.

Steve Farrar writes in his book, *Finishing Strong,* about men being home with their families. He illustrates the point from the life of C.T. Studd—a highly revered name in our Christian heritage. In his day, Studd was the most famous cricket player in all of England. After his conversion, he gave away his entire inheritance and went to the mission field in China. After serving there for a number of years, he returned to England, only to head back out to Africa. Alone.

Leaving his wife behind, C.T. Studd didn't see her again for seventeen years. Candidly, Farrar says, "I'm sorry, but that's weird."[1] I agree. If God brings a woman into your life to be your wife and gives you children, do you think that He would then turn around and call you to forsake them? I don't think so.

I will never forget one evening that I spent with the son of a very famous Christian leader—his father a man so widely known that every one of you would immediately recognize his name.

I was deeply excited for the opportunity to eat dinner with this young man and find out what it was like growing up in such a famous home. But I was not prepared for what I was about to hear. Instead of hearing joy and gratitude,

I heard disappointment and resentment spew out from his mouth. Starving for attention at home, he remained deeply bitter that dad was never there when he was a child. His dad was out winning the world, but losing his own family.

After dinner that night, I went back to my hotel room absolutely stunned. First, because this adult son was still so full of anger and hurt. Second, because I had always wanted to grow up and be like his famous father. But not at this price! I could never afford to lose my own children, no matter how great the ministry. Losing one's children in the process of gaining the world is simply too high a price to pay.

Once back in my hotel room, I dropped to my knees, knelt over my bed, and prayed one of the most serious prayers I've ever prayed in my life. I said, "God, please don't ever let me lose my children in my zeal to win the world." May God answer that prayer!

Men, do you need to spend more time at home? Do you have young kids? If so, they desperately need a daddy and no one else will ever do. Satan offered Christ the kingdoms of this world for one act of compromise. He will cut you a similar deal. Don't buy it!

CHALLENGE #6:
DADS, BE POSITIVE!
Fathers, do not provoke your children to anger.
EPHESIANS 6:4A

A father's words have the power of life and death. They can be either encouraging or crushing, but rarely anything in between. They are able to tear down or build up. Nothing means more to a child than to receive his or her dad's words of acceptance or approval.

Dads, we must recognize our strategic role. What we say to our children must be mostly encouraging, uplifting, affirming, and supportive. Our words must always be weighted toward the positive, never the negative. James Dobson says that we must encourage our children seven times for every one negative or they will grow up thinking that their middle name is, "Sit down and be quiet." When our words are constantly discouraging, we are sowing seeds of resentment deep beneath the surface that will, in due time, yield a harvest of bitterness and estrangement. What the apostle Paul said earlier to the Ephesians must be the watchword for every father. Read these familiar words as though they were addressed directly to you, Dad. "Let no unwholesome word proceed from your mouth, but only such a word as is good for edification according to the need of the moment, that it may give grace to those who hear" (Ephesians 4:29).

What is an "unwholesome word"? The original word in the Greek language *(sapros)* referred to rotten fruit or spoiled food. Thus, an unwholesome word was language that was corrupt or foul. The Bible is saying that no foul speech should ever come from our mouth such as profanity, coarseness, put-downs, cutting sarcasm, meanness, or harmful language. Men, we must never speak like this to our children. Never.

Instead, our words must "only" be edifying. Our speech at home should always be seasoned with salt. It should always build up by being helpful, constructive, and uplifting. Certainly, there will be times when we must be corrective, but even then it must be done in the right spirit.

An edifying word, Paul says, is well chosen "according to the need of the moment." It is uniquely tailored for that specific moment, and should contribute constructively. It never unnecessarily hurts, harms, or wounds a child. Quite frankly, what some dads say at home would be better left unsaid. Even when criticism is spoken, it must always be done in love (Ephesians 4:15) and gentleness (Galatians 6:1).

Edifying words "give grace," providing strength, hope, comfort, consolation, motivation, and assurance.

LET'S GET POSITIVE!

I have made a conscious effort, as a father, to be as positive toward my children as I can possibly be. My father was that way toward me, always affirming me and building me up. In the process, he instilled within me a healthy self-esteem and positive self-confidence. As a result, I grew up being an overachiever who usually got more out of my ability than the next guy simply because of my father's positive words.

As a result, I have endeavored to do the same with my children. I have coached their Little League baseball and Pee Wee basketball teams long enough to know how motivating my encouraging words are. They're like refueling a race car. Words like, "I love you," or "I am so proud of you," or "I know you can do it," rev up their emotional motor and shift them into fifth gear. So do, "I'm so glad you're my child," or "You are so special to me," or

"I can't believe how great you are," or "I love being with you."

Encouraging words feed our children's self-esteem, build their confidence level, and fuel their feeling of personal worth. That's important. Kids who grow up thinking, "I am loved" and "I can do it," usually accomplish more than their share in life. Tragically others grow up thinking, "I am in the way" and "I could never do it." That's why they don't. Their life becomes a self-fulfilled prophecy. These negative life attitudes can be traced back many times to a dad with a defeated attitude himself.

Writing with an insightful pen, Chuck Swindoll puts it this way, "Enhancing your child's self-esteem is next to the greatest contribution you can make in your child's life. The greatest, of course, is helping him cultivate a meaningful, lasting relationship with the living God. Let me put it straight and simple: If your child is launched from your nest secure in Christ and confident he has been designed by God to fulfill a special calling, equipped with the tools to handle the demands of everyday life, you've done your job."[2]

For example, I had a friend, Dave Simmons, with whom I attended Dallas Theological Seminary and Reformed Theological Seminary. We even played on the same intramural basketball team together. As many of you know, Dave was a great athlete, an All-American football player for Georgia Tech, who later played for the Dallas Cowboys. Almost every time I ever heard Dave speak, he referred to his father who never encouraged him. When Dave was named co-captain at the Senior Bowl with Joe Namath, Dave shared that his father told him with a condescending voice, "You couldn't be captain by yourself? Why *only co*-captain?"

After hearing Dave speak several times, each time he referenced this same story. I eventually realized that, even as an adult, Dave had never gotten over his father's lack of emotional support. Although a smashing success in his own life in sports and ministry, he always wrestled with in his dad's lack of encouragement.

Men, discouraging words put a millstone around your child's neck. Always build up their self-confidence and affirm their God-given ability. I am grateful that I grew up in a home where my dad was constantly encouraging me. If I've heard my dad say it once, I've heard him say it a thousand times, "Steve, you can do whatever you put your mind to do." Consequently, I grew up an overachiever who got far more out of my ability than most others who had far greater ability, but less drive and determination, because of my father's positive words.

Be encouraging. It takes no size to criticize.

CHALLENGE #7:
DADS, BE PLIABLE!
Fathers, do not provoke your children to anger.
EPHESIANS 6:4A

Our children resemble us in many ways, emulating both our good points as well as our weaknesses. But they need not completely duplicate the ways of their father in order to be a success. They simply need to be who God designed them to be—no more, no less. As each child grows older, dads should grant greater freedom for individuality.

As I mentioned earlier, I have a framed Norman Rockwell painting that hangs in our home. It is a picture of a father and his son worshipping together in church. They are standing side by side in the same pew, singing from the same hymnal, dressed in the same suit and tie. It is a great painting that portrays family unity and a father and son being bonded together. I believe that children ought to find their role model in their father and desire to emulate their dad in every way that is proper.

But as children grow older, there are different points at which they need to be allowed the freedom to be uniquely themselves. If not, resentment may develop if they feel too confined in certain matters that bear no spiritual or moral significance.

I know of situations where certain children felt so fenced in—bound by a straightjacket of rigid legalism and narrow conformity—that deep resentment began to fester beneath the surface. Roots of bitterness had fertile soil in which to grow. Once that child left home—whether at the time of going to college, or when he or she was married—there was a lot of emotional baggage carried by them into adulthood. The chief reason was because they were never allowed to express themselves individually and be themselves at home. Their fathers ruled with an "If I want your opinion, I'll give it to you" philosophy.

As children enter their teenage years and pass through the rite of puberty, there must be the allowance for some latitude in selected matters such as dress code, hairstyle, room decor, and the like. Such freedom should be allowed only within clearly defined boundaries as long as your child lives under your roof. Unquestionably, certain attire, certain hair lengths, and certain room furnishings are unacceptable. Yet, within the boundaries of what is proper, we, as fathers, must allow for variance and individuality. We must allow our children creativity to color within the defined lines with different colors, according to their individual preferences.

CHALLENGE #8:
DADS, BE PLAYFUL!
Fathers, do not provoke your children to anger.
EPHESIANS 6:4A

A final way that we fathers can provoke our children to anger is by being so serious all the time that we never allow for any fun. Let's face it, we set the mood for our homes. If we're in a bad mood, the entire family has to tiptoe on eggshells. But when we're in a good mood, the whole family picks up the spirit.

Too often, we carry home with us from the office the weight of the world upon our shoulders. Unknowingly, we sometimes even take out our frustrations on our children. If our boss or a customer was too demanding with us at work, we must guard against being that way with our children. If not, the moment we hit the front door, everyone starts scurrying for cover. The Bear is home!

Instead, we must bear the fruit of the Spirit—"love, joy, peace, patience, kindness, goodness, faithfulness, gentleness, self-control" (Galatians 5:22–23). More than anyplace else, the reality of Christ must shine through our lives at home, and this includes a winsome personality that attracts our children to us. You can still attract more flies with honey than with vinegar.

The book of Proverbs was written by Solomon as a collection of the wisdom that he passed down to his children (Proverbs 1:7). In that book—which is very much a timeless manual on child rearing he wrote: "A joyful heart is good medicine" (Proverbs 17:22). And "A joyful heart makes a cheerful face" (Proverbs 15:13). Laughter is contagious and should fill the rooms of our homes.

Solomon also observed, "A time to weep, and a time to laugh, a time to mourn and a time to dance" (Ecclesiastes 3:4). Wise is the father who knows the difference and allows for both. Life is serious enough without making room for some fun and laughter. A little sense of humor goes a long way. A little sugar always helps the medicine go down better.

Have you ever noticed that certain homes tend to be the gathering places in the neighborhood for children? Maybe your home is like that. Maybe your driveway is where the neighborhood kids gather for basketball. Or maybe your den is where your children's friends congregate to watch television. If not, it ought to be. Children want to be where they can have fun. They're smart and can tell where love and laughter fills the house. That's where they want to be. Make your children glad they're a part of your family.

I have made a concerted effort to try to make our family life as fun as it can possibly be. Being in the ministry, we have enough serious moments as it is.

FUN SHOULD BEGIN AT HOME

I'd like to share some of those fun things with you now, and maybe they will help your thinking.

First, *play with your children.* I try to regularly play with my children—football in the front yard, basketball in the driveway, "Clue" in the den, golf at the driving range. Last night, John, my five year old jumped on my back and wanted to wrestle and tickle. Well, once I started pinning him down and tickling him, his laughter brought our other children running. The next thing I knew, the others were trying to pin me down to tickle me. I looked like Gulliver tied down by little people. Men, I can't emphasize this enough—play with your children.

Second, *spend time with your children.* Spending individual time with each child fills up their emotional tank and draws them closer to you. Sometimes I will take our daughter, Grace Anne, on a date. She'll get all dressed up and I'll take her to a fancy hotel restaurant for dessert. Or I'll take John to putt-putt and then get a coke. Or I'll take one or two of them on a walk together. Or we'll go for a bike ride. When I recently bought a bicycle, I bought an infant seat on the back so John could go with me. James and Andrew leave home with me every Sunday morning at 5:50 A.M. and we swing by the doughnut shop on the way to church. Sometimes I'll ask just one of the kids to walk around the block with me and if its one of the boys, we'll take a football and play catch along the way.

Third, *be involved with your children's activities.* To this point, this involvement has been mainly done with our two oldest because of age. I have coached their baseball and basketball teams for third through sixth grades. You talk about fun together! Come by the house and I'll show you the videos of some of our best games. Those are great moments. So are Grace Anne's dance recitals and whatever else they choose to get involved in.

GOD KNOWS BEST

Soon after our recent move to Mobile, Alabama, I asked each of our four children what they liked the most about our new house. I loved what Grace Anne said. After pausing to think for a few seconds, she said, "Dad, what I like most about our new house is our swing on the front porch."

The swing, I thought. What's so hot about that swing? So, I asked her why she liked it so much.

"Dad," she replied, "I love to swing with just you and me on the front porch."

That made me remember what so many people had told me before she was born. I did need a little girl to sit in my lap, to hug on my neck, and to tug on my heart. I needed a little girl to make me a "kinder, gentler" person. I needed a little girl to help me grow in gentleness and kindness.

Yes, God sure knew I needed that little girl. There's power in a father's gentleness.

A young woman relates that when she was a little girl, her father, an artist, would often be busy at his easel, mixing oils and painting on his big canvases while she sat nearby on the floor, working just as hard with her own set of crayons and a coloring book.

Many a time, he would set his brushes aside, reach down, and lift her up onto his lap. Then he'd curl her little hand around one of his brushes, enfolding it with his own larger, stronger hand. And ever so gently, he would guide her hand and the brush, dipping it into the palette and mixing the colors, and then stroke the wet, shiny paint onto the canvas before them both.

Little did this father know that he was giving his daughter skills that would bring great fulfillment to her life. Today, Joni Erickson Tada—a quadriplegic since a diving accident during her teen years—is still painting, but this time with a paintbrush in her mouth. A lot of her earnings are channeled into ministry to help others, and her compassion is a reflection of that shown her by a loving, tender father.

Men, this is the legacy of gentleness we must leave.

CHAPTER 8

I'M NOT RAISIN' CROPS, I'M RAISIN' BOYS

A Legacy of Maturity

IT'S EASIER TO BEND A BOY THAN TO MEND A MAN.

—*Anonymous*

Living on a farm is hard work. And so is leaving a legacy.

I heard about one farmer who lived on a country farm with his four strong, husky teenage boys. From sunrise to sunset, day after day, this farmer could be seen working his four sons, pushing them hard with strenuous labor. It didn't matter what latest technological advances came along in farm equipment, this man refused to purchase any of them because he believed in old-fashioned hard work.

He had a neighbor who owned the farm next to him, who watched in amazement as this farmer put his sons through the grind. Finally, this neighbor couldn't keep quiet any longer. He leaned across the fence and yelled, "Say, you're working your boys too hard. You don't need to work them so hard to raise your crops."

Without missing a beat, the father responded, "I'm not raising *crops,* I'm raising *boys.*"

Men, that's what it's all about. If our kids are going to grow up to be all that God has designed them to be, then we're going to have to get beside them and work hard at seeing them mature and develop.

Crops don't raise themselves.

Neither do children.

Sometimes we wish that our children came out of the box "fully assembled," already mature, and needing very little care. But they don't. They need to be developed in every way—mentally, physically, socially, and spiritually. As fathers, we are entrusted with the weighty responsibility of bringing up our children to be adults who will one day find their place in the world. In this process, one that spans almost two decades, we are to facilitate and encourage their overall growth toward personal maturity.

In all the New Testament, only one verse—Ephesians 6:4, along with its companion verse, Colossians 3:21—speaks *exclusively* to dads and instructs us in the basics of fatherhood. In the last chapter, we looked at the first part of this verse which says, "Fathers do not provoke your children to anger." Now, we want to look at the next part of this key verse which says "but bring them up." Here's how the entire verse reads, "Fathers, do not provoke your children to anger, but bring them up in the discipline and instruction of the Lord" (Ephesians 6:4).

Men, what we are to do with our children is to "bring them up." It is this admonishment, tucked away in the middle of this strategic verse, that I want us to address in this chapter. But before we consider the different ways in which we are to help develop and grow our children, let me make some initial observations about this verse.

First, *fathering requires balance.* You will notice in this verse that there is both a negative and positive command. As dads, there is something we don't do—"do not provoke them to anger"—and something we must do—"bring them up in the discipline and instruction of the Lord." This dual responsibility produces the balance and moderation necessary for successful fathering.

Second, *fathering is to be strongly positive.* When placed on the scales, our fathering should definitely tilt toward the positive. In this verse, there is only one negative command—"do not provoke them to anger"—but three positive requirements—bring them up, discipline them, and instruct them. That tells me our fathering should be strongly weighed to the positive, at least three to one.

Third, *fathering requires tender loving care.* "Bring them up" *(ekrephete)* is a word which means to nourish, or to feed. It is the same word that is translated "nourishes" (Ephesians 5:29), and describes how we should care for our own body. Certainly, no one needs to persuade us to take care of our own personal needs. We naturally do so with care, gentleness, and liberty. That's precisely how we are to love our children. We are to nourish them with a tender care that surrounds them with love.

Fourth, *fathering is an ongoing process.* "Bring them up" is in the present tense, meaning it is a continual process which occurs over many years. As long as our children are under our roof, we are to be directly involved in raising them up from one level of growth to the next. To this day, when my parents hear me preach, they are still helping me with my grammar and the like.

Fifth, *fathering is nonnegotiable.* "Bring them up" is in the imperative mood, meaning it is a command. This verse does not give us advice or suggestions, but an admonishment that is binding. Here is God's authoritative command addressed to every father, a nonnegotiable requiring our obedience.

Sixth, *fathering is every dad's responsibility.* "Bring them up" is in the middle voice, meaning this is our personal responsibility. No one else can bring them up for us. It can not be delegated to a school, day-care center, church, or grandparents. It can not even be solely turned over to mom to do. Raising children is every dad's business. The buck stops with us.

Seventh, *fathering involves developing the whole child.* "Bring them up" has no qualifiers, except with "discipline and instruction." We should involve ourselves in bringing up our children in every area of their lives—all their mental, spiritual, physical, and social aspects. Across the board, fathers must see the big picture and have the overall best interests of their children at heart.

It is along this line of thought that I want to expand this chapter—our fathering involves developing the whole child. "Bring them up" is unqualified and all-inclusive. It involves nurturing the personal growth of the total child. No area is to be left out.

Luke 2:52 defines the basic categories of child development. As it describes the personal growth of the Lord Jesus Himself as a youth, this verse says He "kept increasing in wisdom and stature and in favor with God and man." Each of these four categories—wisdom, stature, God, man—represents an area in which He was brought up and grew toward personal maturity. "Wisdom" refers to His mental development, "stature" means His physical growth, "God" represents His spiritual development, and "man" focuses upon His social development.

Gentlemen, each of these four categories of personal development—the mental, physical, spiritual and social—should be given serious attention as we work with our children. If any one of these areas is overlooked, then our children will be imbalanced and immature. But if healthy growth occurs in all four of these areas, then our children will be progressing toward what God has designed them to be.

With these basic categories to guide our thinking, let's consider now how to "bring them up." The Bible says, "Train up a child in the way he should go and when he is old, he will not depart from it" (Proverbs 22:6, NKJV). As we train up our children, here are the four basic areas of child development.

RESPONSIBILITY #1:
DADS, DEVELOP THEM MENTALLY
Fathers... bring them up.
EPHESIANS 6:4B

Child development begins with the mind. Regarding the critical role of our minds, Solomon observed, "As he thinks within himself, so he is" (Proverbs 23:7). What a person thinks in his heart, or mind, is what he really is. That's because all our decisions, actions, and attitudes flow from the thoughts of our heart. No wonder Solomon said, "Watch over your heart with all diligence, for from it flow the springs of life" (Proverbs 4:23). Our entire life flows out of the thoughts of our heart. What we think is what we are—or will soon become.

Developing our children's minds is of utmost importance and requires that we give them a Christian world view. We want them to see life from God's perspective and gain an understanding of the world around them through the grid of God's truth. Rather than seeing life through the filter of secular humanism—a form of thinking that places man at the center of its world order—we want our children to see through the lens of God's truth as revealed in the Bible—a system of truth which places God at the center of the world order. Bottom line, we must raise them to have a theocentric world view.

As dads, it is our goal to cultivate this Christian mind in our children, one which is thoroughly biblical in its thinking. In Romans 12:2, Paul calls it a renewed mind, one that is enabled to discern and approve God's will. If we want our children to live right, then they must first think right.

In contrast to the secular world around us, a Christian mind is marked by certain biblical truths: a fundamental belief in the existence of God, the recognition of moral absolutes, the acceptance of divine authority, the dignity of human life in God's image, the fall of mankind, the redemption that is in Christ, and man's eternal destiny in heaven or hell. That is the Christian world view that we want to see flourish in the minds of our children.

HOME, CHURCH, AND SCHOOL

In order to develop such a distinctly Christian mind in our children, we must educate them and that involves three key arenas—the home, the church, and the school. I want us to give thought now to each of these areas.

First, *developing a Christian mind begins at home.* All the influences of a Christian home must be brought to bear upon our children to produce a consistent Christian world view. This involves the teaching of mom and dad, the books and videos made available, the forms of entertainment pursued, the music listened to, the guests received, the friends made, and the conversations engaged. All these should come together to form one *coherent* body of truth that is set before our children.

When I lived in Little Rock, a scientist explained to me what "coherent" means. Drawing from the world of laser technology, he described how a laser beam of light is coherent. Rather than being dispersed particles of light, the laser beam is tightly focused and precise. It is coherent. Doctors use the laser beam in surgery because of its pinpoint accuracy. That's what "coherent" truth is. Like a focused laser beam, a Christian world view is defined, narrow, and determined.

The learning environment that we provide for our children should be coherent as it lines up with the Word of God. We must monitor all influences that come into our homes that do not square with Scripture. Not much television is Christian, and not everyone who comes into our homes will be Christian, yet we must control these influences and point out to our children when and where they depart from biblical absolutes.

I do not advocate children watching much television, but if they do see something, such as the news, that represents a humanistic philosophy, we should give them the scriptural frame of reference and point out where that teaching went astray. In so doing, we will be teaching our kids to think critically rather than naively. If someone visits our home who espouses a worldly mind set, then that error needs to be corrected in our children's thinking.

Before we moved to Mobile, we lived in Little Rock, Arkansas, for fourteen years. During that time, we saw a lot about the Clintons on television. Now I must tell you that I agree with very little about their political and moral positions. Their agenda was constantly coming into our home as we were watching television together. There was many an evening when I had to reeducate our children after we had heard a news report and explain to them God's perspective on the issue just addressed. And at the same time, we also needed to be reminded of the respect we must show the office of president.

Dads, we must be constantly teaching our children at home. Over the sink in our kitchen, Anne has a verse mounted for us all to see and be reminded, "We are taking every thought captive to the obedience of Christ" (2 Corinthians 10:5). That's what we must be always doing, not only for ourselves, but for our children. We are to measure every thought by the standard of God's Word, and bring it into alignment with Christ.

Second, *developing a Christian mind extends to school.* What we teach at home should be reinforced at school—not contradicted. We don't want our children receiving a mixed signal sent between home and school. That would be "incoherent." Instead, as best it can be established, we want one body of truth taught from the bedroom to the classroom. Consequently, where our children attend school should be a matter of great concern for every father, and requires our careful consideration.

Regarding our children's formal education, there are basically four options before us—public school, private school, Christian school, and home school. In my estimation, there is no one correct solution for every family. God must lead each dad individually to answer this issue for himself. Amid the various considerations, we must ask ourselves: Where will my child be best developed *mentally? Physically? Spiritually? Socially?*

While each of these areas must be considered, the mental and spiritual must take priority over the physical and social. And our children's inner life must take precedence over their outer life.

Dads, are you involved *where* your children are attending school? Are you aware of *what* is being taught? Have you examined the curriculum and text books? Is school reinforcing what you are teaching at home? Or, is school competing against what you're teaching? *How* are your children doing? Do you see them making progress as they should?

Third, *developing a Christian mind involves church. Where* we attend church, and *how* we involve our family in church, are also very important to the mental development of our children. As dads, we must consider what effect our church is having upon a consistent Christian world view being set before our children.

Does our church develop our kids biblically? Are the truths being taught on Sunday supporting and enhancing what you are teaching at home? Is what is being taught relevant, practical, and positive? Are the children and student ministries grounded in God's truth? Is the pulpit ministry and worship alive, uplifting, and biblical?

In developing our children mentally, each of these three areas must be considered—*home, school,* and *church.* Dads, it is our responsibility to oversee the overall education in these areas and coordinate them into one common pursuit of truth in a way that is life changing for our children.

RESPONSIBILITY #2:
DADS, DEVELOP THEM PHYSICALLY!
Fathers...bring them up.
EPHESIANS 6:4B

Fathers also have the responsibility to provide all that is necessary for their children's physical growth. This involves providing the basics of life—food, shelter, clothing, medical care, exercise, and the like. Actually, this is the primary meaning of the word "bring up." It refers to providing your children with the financial support and necessary opportunities needed for their physical welfare.

First, *dads should provide financially for their children.* The Bible says, "If anyone does not provide for his own, and especially for those of his household, he has denied the faith, and is worse than an unbeliever" (1 Timothy 5:8). This means that fathers must work hard at providing a living for their family. Dads are to be the breadwinner and put food on the table, as well as whatever else his family needs to pursue God's will for their lives.

Thus, dads should work hard in order to earn a living and provide for his family's needs. "The laborer is worthy of his wages" (1 Timothy 5:18). In addition to meeting his children's basic needs, loving fathers will want to provide "extras" as well, such as an occasional special gift, toys, sporting equipment, vacation, or the like. All this will vary depending upon a dad's earning power and lifestyle.

Two extremes should be avoided here. The first danger is the tendency to overindulge our children and provide *too many* extras for them. In the process, we spoil them, and they grow up thinking that everything will fall into their laps. Worse, such pampering will feed a corrupting materialism. Children should have their needs met, but not their greeds.

Many fathers today want to provide a better lifestyle for their children than the one in which they grew up, and in the process, their own children grow up knowing the price of everything, but the value of nothing. Restraint and moderation should be exhibited by doting dads.

The other extreme is to fail to provide what our children need, especially if you are able, or to withhold occasional generosity. Some dads are so tight they squeak. They think buying underwear at a "Blue Light Special" at Kmart is splurging. Sometimes dads are frugal because they grew up in a meager background. But other dads are "cheap" and don't want to spend money for toys and such things because they could be spending it on themselves.

Second, *dads should encourage their children in physical exercise.* Personally, I feel that every father should encourage each child to participate in one sport or another. Recently, I recounted to my father the benefits that I gained as a child from participating in sports. I am very grateful that he encouraged me to pursue sports because it was an essential part of my personal development; its benefits have stayed with me to this day.

Through athletics, I learned qualities like character, dedication, and self-discipline. Along with these, I learned the ability to work on a team, a tough-mindedness to endure, how to bounce back from defeat, an ability to function under pressure, and a submission to authority. Likewise, I learned character issues like fortitude, humility, how to be gracious in victory, and the value of training and preparation. I also learned through sports the virtues of leadership, self-control, being focused, overcoming opposition, blocking out distractions, playing hurt, how to be a leader, and the necessity of playing by rules. Through my physical participation in sports, I was stretched in ways that have benefited my spiritual life.

When the Pulpit Committee from Mobile first talked to me, they asked me how I had been able to pastor one church for fourteen years. I said I learned a mental toughness in athletics that you never give up under adversity. We had a sign in our football locker room which said, "When the Going Gets Tough the Tough Get Going." It was drilled into me that when it's third and 15, or fourth and 5, and you're near the goal line, you dig in and hang tough. You do what it takes to win.

Applying this disciplined mind set, we must not allow our children to grow up to be "couch potatoes." Fathers who do should be reprimanded. Their kids never exercise, but lounge around at home all day, watching television or playing Nintendo games, while munching on potato chips. Their bodies more resemble bowls of Jell-O than growing muscles. If a child is to develop physically, dads must require their children to exercise, stay trim, and be disciplined.

For our family, biking has become a pastime that we enjoy together. We enjoy walking together, playing basketball together and—I don't know if I've ever mentioned this—playing golf together. No couch potatoes allowed here!

Third, *dads should oversee the eating habits of their children.* It is our responsibility to make sure that they are properly fed and nourished. This may have been an unnecessary word several years ago, but today's trend toward junk food and eating disorders make it timely. This may require that we be willing to alter our own diet if we are to set the proper example at home.

Not that I have much room to talk about this. It's a wonder I didn't send my father to an early grave over my eating. As a child growing up, I only ate from the three basic food groups—McDonald's, Wendy's, and Burger King. My "selective" eating stays with me to this day. In fact, I have "coherent" eating—its defined, narrow, and determined! For some of us dads who have a son or daughter like I was, it will require a little extra persuasion, creativity, and much patience.

Fourth, *dads should provide proper medical care.* This, too, is a part of "nourishing" our children. I never realized the importance of this until I became the father of young children. The family pediatrician plays an indispensable role in the proper health care of your children, especially your little ones.

One year we figured up that we (or should I say, Anne) made fifty-six trips to the pediatrician's office. That's more than one trip a week, but it was necessary for our children's physical care. And it came at a price.

All four of these aspects are a part of dads developing their children physically—financial resources, physical exercise, proper food, and medical care.

RESPONSIBILITY #3:
DADS, DEVELOP THEM SPIRITUALLY!
Fathers...bring them up.
EPHESIANS 6:4B

Just as Jesus grew "in favor with God" (Luke 2:42), so should our children. We must encourage the same spiritual development in our young ones and nurture them in the same pursuit of godliness. Dad is the family shepherd who must lead his flock into a deeper knowledge of God, which will transform their lives.

Men, this is our responsibility. What should we do?

First, *help your children develop a heart for God.* More than anything else, you want them to have a heart for God. This begins when our children take a step of faith in their heart and believe that Christ is God's Son who died for their sins and rose again. He must be real in their heart, but that's only the beginning.

Day by day, we want our children to grow in their love for Christ. The greatest commandment, Jesus said, is that we love God with all our heart, soul, mind, and strength (Matthew 22:37). Unlike the Pharisees, who honored God with their lips but whose hearts were far from Him, we desire our children to have a genuine heart for God.

What does a heart for God look like?

The other day while searching for my Bible, I picked up Grace Anne's by mistake. Opening it, I came upon a passage from which I had recently preached. Imagine the excitement in my heart as I discovered my sermon notes written in the margin of her Bible. I then found her sermon notebook with careful notes recorded in it. It's not typical for a third grader to give such careful attention to the proclamation of God's Word. I tell you, that's a heart devoted to God—and I'm grateful.

Let's face it, our children will develop a heart for God when we, as dads, model it before them. Faith is as much caught as it is taught. Whatever is our focus, our passion, and our love will be theirs. That's never more true than in passing down a legacy of maturity.

Dads, when our children see us devoted to prayer, they will pray. When they see us hungering for God's Word, they, too, will desire the pure milk of the Word. When they see enthusiastic service for God, they, too, will seek to serve Him. And when they see us sacrificially loving others, they, too, will be challenged to show love. When we purpose in our heart, "But as for me and my house, we will serve the Lord" (Joshua 24:15), their spiritual maturity will be the inevitable legacy.

Just Say No!

Second, *help your children resist the lure of the world.* We have to train them to say "no" to temptation before they leave the safe, protected haven of our homes. That requires teaching them the difference between good and evil, as well as the high value of standing firm against the seductive pull of this godless world system. We must equip them to stand alone, to cut against the grain, and to swim against the tide of popular culture.

These are days of unparalleled departure from biblical absolutes and our children are caught in a cross fire of competing values. They are being bombarded from every angle—the media, school, society, and their peers. And it starts when they're barely out of the crib with the lure of the newest toys, cartoons, game boards, television shows, and video games. It moves into the areas of the latest fashions, pop music, and school lingo. Don't ever forget Madison Avenue, Hollywood, and MTV are all a part of Satan's system that is trying to recruit and ruin our kids.

Dads, have *we* said no to the world?

Have we instructed our *kids* to resist the lure of the world?

Take, for example, our boys who have come home wanting me to buy them the latest athletic shoes on the market. They've seen other guys at school sporting that new footwear, or because they see a flashy advertisement, it makes them want them as well. But, I've had to tell to them that just because everyone else is wearing the newest hightop, high-tech, pump-up, air-out, light-up shoe doesn't mean that we're going to remortgage our house to bankroll buying these expensive shoes. Instead, we have set a spending cap and let them pick out basketball shoes within a reasonable price limit.

We must point out to them the sheer vanity and utter futility of buying into this world's system. It's like purchasing stock in a bankrupt company. It's like jumping onto a sinking ship—it's not going anywhere fast but down. This world crucified the Lord Jesus Christ. How can we be a friend of this world that put Him to death?

While the world is trying to establish entrance into our children's hearts, we must teach them that, as Christians, they are strangers and aliens here. Their citizenship is in heaven, and while they are in the world, they are not of the world.

I tell my children when they misbehave, "You're a Lawson. If you're going to be a Lawson, you don't act that way." How much more so is that true regarding our sonship in God's family. Because they are God's children, they are to live and act in a way that reflects who they are in Christ.

RESPONSIBILITY #4:
DADS, DEVELOP THEM SOCIALLY!
Fathers... bring them up.
EPHESIANS 6:4B

Finally, we fathers have the responsibility to see that our children develop socially. This means teaching them how to function effectively in society and get along with other people. This involves creating a home environment where interpersonal relationships and manners are taught and modeled which will carry over to other aspects of their lives—and hopefully will stick with them.

What can we do to promote social graces?

First, *teach them to use proper etiquette.* When meeting adults, we want to teach our children to look them in the eye, shake their hand firmly, and speak clearly without mumbling. Teaching courtesy includes instructing our children to open the door for ladies and older adults, as well as allowing them to go through it first. When older children are seated, they should be taught to rise when an adult enters the room or approaches the dinner table.

As I've mentioned in an earlier chapter, let me remind you again. Our children should be taught to address adults as "Mr." or "Mrs." In our day, we've gotten way too lax about allowing our children to address adults by their first name as if they're on the same level. Respect for others is expressed in personal etiquette. Also, we should teach them proper appreciation for courtesies received by saying "Thank you."

Second, *teach them to dress properly.* Regarding their appearance, young people should not look like an unmade bed. How they dress is reflective of their heart's attitude. In public, sloppy dress is often indicative of an indifferent heart. Offbeat dress is usually reflective of a rebellious life. By contrast, a well-groomed and neat appearance usually indicates a respectful attitude. Being appropriately dressed shows regard for adults and authority.

I believe boys ought to look like young men and girls ought to look like young ladies. The Bible is dead set against the unisex movement today which seeks to blur any noticeable differences between the sexes. Let me say it again, boys ought to look like young men and girls ought to look like young ladies. At the risk of sounding legalistic, I want to say that unless your occupation is that of a pirate, young men ought not to wear earrings.

Along another line, modesty may not be in vogue in Paris, or selling in New York, but it is still in style in heaven. Young ladies must be taught to dress discreetly without drawing undue attention to their body in an enticing way. The Bible says, "I want women to adorn themselves with proper clothing, modestly, and discreetly" (1 Timothy 2:9). Our bodies are the temple of the Holy Spirit of God and ought to be properly adorned.

Third, *teach them proper hygiene.* As crazy as this sounds, and I'll have to admit I can't believe I went to seminary for eight years to tell you this, dads, we need to teach our kids to brush their teeth, properly bathe, comb their hair, wear clean clothes, and use deodorant. As elementary as this sounds, this is a part of raising your children to be socially acceptable.

Fourth, *teach them to interact with other people.* As dads, we must also teach our children how to converse and get along with other people without being needlessly offensive. Abrasive language, crude stories, ill-aimed humor, and ethnic prejudice should have no place in the lives of our children. At the same time, we should also teach them not to dominate conversations, but to ask questions to draw others into the discussion. And sarcasm should have its limits and know its place. Again, this cuts against the grain of the world in which our children live.

This is no big incident, but the other night we were leaving our boys' basketball game. It had turned very cold that evening and one of our boys had no sweat shirt or jacket to wear home. Because it was very cold, Anne threw her winter coat over his bare shoulders as they headed out of the gym. Going to the car, a little girl about our boy's age taunted him, "Ahhhhh, you look like a girl."

Looking at our son's face, we could tell he felt put down.

To which Anne wheeled around and responded to this child, "Young lady, you are totally out of line. You shouldn't say anything like that. This isn't your concern." I'm glad she did.

This is just a small example of what our kids face. Children can be mean to one another. We must teach them how to handle this, but more importantly, how not to do it themselves.

The Golden Rule should always be in effect. "However you want people to treat you, so treat them" (Matthew 7:12). As the old saying goes, "If you don't have anything good to say about someone, don't say it at all." This is more than just your words, its your actions and attitudes as well. Teach them to be kind and friendly in all their contacts.

All this is to say that we have a tremendous responsibility to our children to help them grow up. We are assigned by God to prepare them to live successfully in the world. Success for our children requires that they function effectively in every area of their life—mentally, physically, spiritually, and socially. No one area can be neglected, or the result will be an imbalanced, even dysfunctional, young person. But if we bring up our children in each of these aspects of life, we can be confident that they will be well equipped to be used by God for whatever purpose He has intended for them.

Are your children *growing* and *developing*? Are they growing *wiser* and *smarter*? Are they growing *stronger* and *healthier*? Are they growing *deeper* and *closer* to God? Are they growing *kinder* and *gentler*?

In everything we do for our children, there must be one underlying purpose. We want them to be trained to be the spiritual champions that God created them to be. If we can follow the direction of the truths discussed in this chapter, a legacy of maturity will be built into their lives that will cause them to be "brought up" to be winners in life.

CHAPTER 9

IT ALL STARTS AT THE "BOTTOM"

A Legacy of Discipline

TOO MANY PARENTS ARE NOT ON SPANKING TERMS WITH THEIR CHILDREN.
—*Anonymous*

Leaving a legacy requires applying discipline. Without it, a father's instruction is mere advice.

When my son Andrew was five years old, he disobeyed me in a particular matter and I sent him to his room for a spanking. When I walked into the bedroom, I was shocked to find out that a revival meeting had *mysteriously* broken out. He was kneeling over his bed, hands folded, face turned heavenward, praying out loud—for me to hear—confessing his sins and claiming his forgiveness.

Somehow, I felt the sincerity of his repentance was more attached to a keen sense of self-preservation than to any genuine conviction.

As I started to spank Andrew, I noticed that he had *strangely* added about twenty pounds to his small frame. Amazing for a five-year-old child! As it turned out, he put on four pairs of underwear before I could get to his room. A few handkerchiefs were stuffed into his back pockets. If only he could have been this ingenious in order to obey me. I have to admit I did everything I could to hold back laughing. It's not easy to spank the Pillsbury doughboy when you're trying to suppress laughter.

And then there was the time when I laid our youngest son John across my lap to spank him. He was wriggling around so badly that I felt like I was mud wrestling a live alligator. As I tried to spank him, I completely missed him and nailed myself, but in this particular case, it *really* did hurt *me* more than it hurt him.

As a child growing up, my dad used to tell me, "Son, this is going to hurt me more than it hurts you." I always wanted to reply, "Then I'd hate to see you suffer so. Why don't we swap roles and let me give *you* the spanking." For some reason, I never worked up my courage to make that offer. If I had, I'm sure I would have heard, "Son, I brought you *into* this world, and I can take you *out.*"

My dad also used to say, "Son, I'm only spanking you because I love you." If so, he loved me more than he loved my brother and sister. I bore the proof.

In this chapter, I want to talk about leaving a legacy of discipline. Children need more than instruction. There must also be discipline. Giving instruction without discipline is merely giving advice. Kids need to learn very early that wrong decisions lead to painful consequences. Every sin has a price. Pain administered through discipline is a persuasive teacher that delivers the truth home to a child's heart. Every child needs discipline. Without it, their lives are lived without the self-control required to function effectively in whatever God calls them to do.

What is the purpose of discipline? *Why* are we to discipline our children? *How* are we to discipline our children?

DAD IS THE KEY

Every father must master the art of discipline. The Bible clearly calls for dads to carry out biblical discipline, and to fail to do so is to fall short of what God requires of us. But if we will apply loving discipline as the Scriptures teach, our children will grow up to be what God desires. Let's look again at our key verse:

> And fathers, do not provoke your children to anger, but bring them
> up in the discipline and instruction of the Lord. (Ephesians 6:4)

Before we get into the heart of this chapter, I want to bring to your attention five key observations about discipline that emerge from this verse.

First, *fathers are to be the primary disciplinarians.* Paul says, "Fathers... bring them up in the discipline...of the Lord." This is because dads are the spiritual leaders at home. Whenever we are at home, we ought to be the one to carry out the discipline. When we are at work or away from home, the responsibility of discipline is delegated to our wives. But discipline, nevertheless, remains our ultimate responsibility as dads. The buck always stops with us.

Second, *fathers are to carry out discipline on God's behalf.* This verse say it's "the discipline…of the Lord" that we implement, not our own. We are God's representatives, administering God's discipline. We stand in His place to bring about the discipline that He requires. Thus, every earthly father is an extension of our heavenly Father in the matter of discipline.

Third, *fathers must be under control when they exercise discipline.* This verse appeals to fathers to not "provoke your children to anger" in carrying out discipline. As men, we can have a tendency to be too demanding, too impatient with our children. So, God calls for self-restraint when we discipline our children. We must have discipline when we administer discipline.

Fourth, *fathers must surround discipline with instruction.* This verse couples together "the discipline and instruction of the Lord." Discipline and instruction must always go hand in hand. Instruction should both precede discipline as well as follow it. First, we should teach what is expected *before* discipline is ever applied. And we should teach after discipline is applied so that the wrong will not be repeated.

Fifth, *fathers should consider discipline to be very important.* The mere fact that this verse mentions discipline makes it very significant. Paul could have included any number of things in this verse about how to raise our children. Anything listed here should be considered of the utmost importance. Consequently, the fact that discipline is mentioned here—the only verse, along with Colossians 3:21, in the entire New Testament addressed exclusively to fathers—makes a significant statement and begs for our attention.

With this as a brief introduction, let's now consider more specifically what discipline is and how and when to apply it. Without discipline, our children will remain spiritually immature, socially unbalanced, and emotionally insecure. It is an absolutely essential part of their child development.

CHALLENGE #1:
DADS, UNDERSCORE DISCIPLINE!
Fathers…bring them up in the discipline…of the Lord.
EPHESIANS 6:4

The place to begin is to understand the role of discipline. In this verse, the word "discipline" is a Greek word *(paideia)* which comes from the word *(pais)* for children. It refers to the systematic training of sons and daughters to bring them to maturity. In it's broadest extent, the word encompasses all that parents do to teach and train their children. In it's more narrow sense, it refers to a father's correction or punishment for wrongdoing, including the infliction of pain.

In order to gain a better understanding of what discipline is, let's look briefly at another key passage, Hebrews 12:5–11, where the word "discipline" is used nine times. Although this passage describes God's discipline of us, His children, the truth nevertheless applies to every father as we discipline our children. How God disciplines us is how we should discipline our children. Here's what the Scripture says:

> And you have forgotten the exhortation which is addressed to you as sons, "MY SON, DO NOT REGARD LIGHTLY THE DISCIPLINE OF THE LORD, NOR FAINT WHEN YOU ARE REPROVED BY HIM; FOR THOSE WHOM THE LORD LOVES HE DISCIPLINES, AND HE SCOURGES EVERY SON WHOM HE RECEIVES." It is for discipline that you endure; God deals with you as with sons; for what son is there whom his father does not discipline? But if you are without discipline of which all have become partakers, then you are illegitimate children and not sons. Furthermore, we had earthly fathers to discipline us, and we respected them; shall we not much rather be subject to the Father of spirits, and live? For they disciplined us for a short time as seemed best to them, but He disciplines us for our good, that we may share His holiness. All discipline for the moment seems not to be joyful, but sorrowful; yet to those who have been trained by it, afterwards it yields the peaceful fruit of righteousness. (Hebrews 12:5–11)

In this passage, Hebrews 12:5–6 is a direct quote from Proverbs 3:11–12, where Solomon instructs his own sons about accepting God's discipline. This tells me fathers have long instructed their sons in the matter of receiving discipline. From these verses, I want us to consider carefully God's discipline because it should lead us in disciplining our own children. Notice now eight truths about discipline from this passage:

EIGHT TRUTHS ABOUT DISCIPLINE

First, *discipline is to be taken seriously* (verse 5). This passage calls us to "not regard lightly the discipline of the Lord." Although painful to receive, it is a necessary aspect of growing up and personal maturity. Similarly, a father's discipline in the home is to be taken seriously. Any father who fails to discipline his children fails to take God's Word seriously. We must never question it's importance, nor be careless in carrying it out.

Second, *discipline demonstrates a father's love* (verse 6). This passage says, "Those whom the Lord loves He disciplines." God's correction proves He cares for us. He loves us just as we are, but too much to let us *remain* the way we are because He seeks to make us the very best that we can possibly be, which is Christlike. Similarly, a father's love is proven by his discipline. Sometimes, I hear a dad say, "I love my child too much to discipline him." Not so. If he loved him or her, he would discipline them. The reason that he doesn't discipline is because he loves himself too much to be troubled or get involved. The Bible says, "He who spares his rod hates his son, but he who loves him disciplines him diligently" (Proverbs 13:24).

Third, *discipline involves both verbal and physical correction* (verses 5–6). This passage says that we are not to "faint when you are reproved by Him…and He scourges every son whom He receives." Here is mentioned both verbal correction ("reproof") and physical punishment ("scourging"). These two expressions—reproof and scourging—cover both ends of discipline. It starts as a verbal reproof, but may escalate to a physical scourging if one's disobedience continues.

In like manner, fathers are to give both a verbal rebuke as well as physical punishment, depending upon the seriousness of the wrong committed. The punishment should fit the crime. Lesser wrongs and first time offenses require merely a rebuke. But greater wrongs and repeat offenses may require the infliction of physical pain through a spanking. We will talk later in this chapter about when and how to apply which form of discipline.

Fourth, *discipline must be painful if it is to be effective* (verses 5–6). To be "reproved" by the Lord through His Word and to receive His "scourging" through painful circumstances, as Hebrews 12 teaches, is never pleasant. If God's discipline is to get our attention, it must be painful. So, a father's chastisement should be painful. We are instructed, "Do not hold back discipline from the child, although you beat him with the rod, he will not die"

(Proverbs 23:13). Our rebuke must sting, our rod must inflict pain.

Fifth, *discipline is a proof of genuine sonship* (verses 7–8). This says, "It is for discipline that you endure. God deals with you as with sons. For what son is there for whom the Father does not discipline?" It is a rhetorical question that implies a negative answer. It is so obvious that God does not even bother to answer it. Of course, fathers discipline their children. He says, "If you are without discipline of which all have become partakers, then you are illegitimate children and not sons." Quite simply, no discipline, no sonship. Picture five boys out playing in the front yard, and all five are misbehaving. Two of them are your sons. If you go out and stop the ruckus, I can tell you which two are yours. It will be the two who are disciplined, not the other three. The two are your direct responsibility.

Sixth, *discipline produces respect toward fathers* (verse 9). God says, "Therefore, we have earthly fathers to discipline us, and we respected them." Discipline has a sobering effect that causes children to take their father seriously. It breeds a healthy fear of God in their hearts. Conversely, the surest way to lose a child's respect is to never correct or punish him or her.

Seventh, *the pain of discipline is only temporary* (verses 10–11). The Bible says "They disciplined us for a short time… All discipline for the moment seems not to be joyful." Discipline ought to be short-lived, because we ought to be learning the lesson and changing our behavior. The same ought to be true with our fathering toward our children. Discipline ought to be short-lived and infrequent.

Obviously, there are times, depending upon the age of our children, when discipline must be more regular, especially in their earlier years. Admittedly, there were times with my children when it resembled a standoff. But that was the exception, not the rule. Like a doctor in surgery, the time for operating should be short-lived, but yield long-term, positive results.

Eighth, *discipline is life changing* (verses 10–11). This passage says, "He disciplines us for our good, that we may share His holiness to those who have been trained by it, afterwards it yields the peaceful fruit of righteousness." God's discipline does in fact work, bringing about a change of heart and separating us from our sin, because the pain of God's discipline becomes greater than the pleasure derived from our sin. In like manner, our discipline should remove from our children's heart the desire for wrong choices. Like the surgeon's scalpel that cuts deeply solely to bring healing to the body, our discipline inflicts pain, but only to bring holiness in the lives of our children.

Here's what we must understand about a father's discipline. As seen from Hebrews 12:5–11, our discipline must be: (1) taken seriously, (2) applied lovingly, (3) varied, (4) painful, (5) revealing, (6) instructive, and (7) temporary if it is to be (8) life changing. If we are to leave a legacy with our children, then we must grasp these essential truths.

CHALLENGE #2:
DADS, UNDERSTAND DISCIPLINE!
Fathers…bring them up in the discipline…of the Lord.
EPHESIANS 6:4

Now that we better understand the importance of discipline, the second challenge we face is to know the various forms of discipline and when to apply each. The punishment must fit the crime. Consequently, we must always strive to be fair and just in carrying out our discipline. Too harsh of a punishment unnecessarily provokes a child to anger. Too lenient of a punishment fails to deal properly with the wrong committed. Wise is the father who knows when to administer which punishment.

Broadly speaking, there are six stages of corrective discipline that can be applied, depending upon the age of the child and the nature of the wrong committed. From the least painful to the most painful, these are: (1) verbal correction, (2) withholding privileges, (3) natural consequences, (4) isolation, (5) assigning responsibilities, and (6) spanking. We must know when to apply each. Let's briefly consider each one:

First, *verbal correction.* Stage one is our verbal correction. This would be either a gentle rebuke, stinging reprimand, or stern warning depending upon the wrong committed. This form of discipline should be used with minor infractions and first time offenses. This is exactly how God disciplines us. When we read His Word, the Bible, it stings, rebukes, reproves, and corrects us (2 Timothy 3:16).

Likewise, our words should correct our children when they do wrong and carry a convicting force about them. Certainly, we must be always careful to speak the truth in love (Ephesians 4:16) without allowing our words to be filled with harsh anger.

Second, *withholding privileges*. Stage two of discipline is withholding privileges from our children. God does this with us in our Christian life. Our disobedience often causes us to sacrifice God's blessing and may even disqualify us from participating in various aspects of ministry (1 Corinthians 9:27). Israel's unbelief in the wilderness caused God to withhold privileges from them, such as entering into the Promised Land for forty years (Hebrews 3:13; 4:6). Moses struck the rock in anger and God withheld his privilege to enter the Promised Land (Numbers 20:1–12).

In like manner, we should discern when it is appropriate to withhold privileges from our children for certain lesser wrongs committed. This may include holding back certain activities such as dessert, playing, or watching television. When carefully selected, a withheld privilege can be a very effective means of punishment that gets a child's attention.

Third, *natural consequences*. A next stage of discipline is, in a sense, doing nothing. It is when a father allows his child to experience the natural consequences of his wrong choices. Instead of bailing the child out of trouble, the best punishment may be to allow him or her to suffer the natural consequences of the wrong choice. Certain wrong actions produce their own painful consequences. Paul called it the law of sowing and reaping (Galatians 6:7) in which one reaps *what* one sows. Suffering the consequences of a wrong decision becomes a great teacher not to do it again.

For instance, we explain to our children at the beginning of each school year that if they forget to take their lunch or homework to school, we will not bring it to them. As much as we want them to eat and make good grades, a greater good is involved. They must learn responsibility at an early age or suffer the consequences. Admittedly, there are exceptions under unusual circumstances, but we also need to be careful not to be always bailing them out of trouble.

Fourth, *isolation*. The next stage of discipline is to send the child into isolation, such as to their room. We are social beings who enjoy contact with other people. To be deprived of fun interaction with others is usually unenjoyable. Sometimes, God uses isolation as a stricter form of punishment with us. For example, if we will not repent and turn from our sin, we may be put out of the church and treated like a "Gentile or tax gatherer" (Matthew 18:15–18). Similarly, isolation is a form of punishment that can be used by fathers with their children.

Fifth, *additional work*. Another stage of discipline takes the form of assigning our children additional work. God Himself disciplined Israel when they failed to obey Him, resulting in the additional work of wandering in the wilderness for forty years. God said concerning their wilderness wanderings, "They shall not enter My rest" (Hebrews 4:3).

Similarly, a father may choose to assign a child extra work around the house such as cleaning out the garage, raking leaves, folding laundry, washing windows, vacuuming the carpet, and other such "chores." Recently, our four children were sent upstairs to clean their rooms, but not long afterward, it sounded like a herd of elephants stampeding upstairs. Instead of obeying what I had asked them to do, they were playing tag. So, their punishment was additional work—to fold a mountain of clothes. You might say I took them to the cleaners!

Sixth, *spanking*. Finally, spanking is reserved for major offenses committed such as deliberate disobedience or a defiant attitude. The biblical term "chastisement" means to inflict pain for the purpose of changing wrong attitudes or actions. The book of Proverbs has much to say about spanking, or chastisement. The following verses contain the wise observations of fathers who are on target with their kids:

He who spares his rod hates his son. But he who loves him, disciplines him diligently. (Proverbs 13:24)

Foolishness is bound up in the heart of a child; the rod of discipline will remove it far from him. (Proverbs 22:15)

Do not hold back discipline from the child, although you beat him with the rod, he will not die. You shall beat him with the rod and deliver his soul from Sheol. (Proverbs 23:13–14)

The rod and reproof give wisdom, but a child who gets his own way brings shame to his mother. Correct your son, and he will give you comfort; he will also delight your soul. (Proverbs 29:15, 17)

In each of these verses, the rod is a clear reference to the physical pain applied to a child's buttocks in the case of deliberate disobedience or defiance.

Today, we call this spanking. A clear distinction needs to be made between biblical spanking and child abuse. Since ours is a day of extremes, Chuck Swindoll provides us with some helpful contrasts.[1]

ABUSE	DISCIPLINE
Unfair and unexpected	Fair and expected
Degrading and demoralizing	Upholds dignity
Extreme—too harsh, brutal	Balanced—within limits
Torturous—leaves scars	Painful—but leaves no scars
Results from hatred and resentment	Prompted by love and concern
Creates terror, emotional damage, and resentment of authority	Leads to healthy respect for authority
Destroys self-esteem; leads to horrifying, permanent damage and the inability later in life to maintain responsibilities	Strengthens self-esteem; leads to the individual's ability to later discipline himself

Noting many of the same differences, Gary and Anne Marie Ezzo contrast the abuses of spanking today with biblical chastisement.

CULTURAL SPANKING is something parents do to a child.
BIBLICAL CHASTISEMENT is something parents do for a child.

CULTURAL SPANKING is a reaction activated by frustration.
BIBLICAL CHASTISEMENT is a response activated by rebellion.

CULTURAL SPANKING is used as a punishment of last resort.
BIBLICAL CHASTISEMENT is not an act of punishment but of love.

CULTURAL SPANKING attempts to change outward behavior.
BIBLICAL CHASTISEMENT is used to change inward attitudes.

CULTURAL SPANKING is used with the intent to punish behavior.

BIBLICAL CHASTISEMENT is used with the intent to amend behavior.

CULTURAL SPANKING is performed throughout a child's life.
BIBLICAL CHASTISEMENT is nearly completed by the age of five.

CULTURAL SPANKING frustrates the child.
BIBLICAL CHASTISEMENT clears a child's guilty conscience.

CULTURAL SPANKING has no long-term positive effect.
BIBLICAL CHASTISEMENT molds lifelong character.

CULTURAL SPANKING is used by most Christians.
BIBLICAL CHASTISEMENT is rarely used by anyone.[2]

These differences should be clearly understood.

CHALLENGE # 3:
DADS UNDERTAKE DISCIPLINE!
Fathers...bring them up in the discipline...of the Lord.
EPHESIANS 6:4

Having drawn a careful distinction between the proper and improper uses of spanking, let me share several key steps in spanking if it is to be used successfully.

First, *start early.* The practice of chastisement should begin as soon as a child can differentiate between right and wrong. The Bible says, "Foolishness is bound up in the heart of a child; the rod of discipline will remove it far from him" (Proverbs 22:15). This word for "child" means one as young as an infant or older. Scripture says, "He who spares his rod hates his son, but he who loves him disciplines him diligently" (Proverbs 13:24). That word "diligently" means at dawn, or early in the day. It is a figure of speech that means early in life. That's when discipline should begin—early.

At what age should you begin spanking? That all depends upon the emotional and psychological development of your child. With our boys, we began slapping their hand when they were nine months old, and spanking their bottom at fourteen months of age. With our little girl, she was ten months when we started slapping her hand and sixteen months when we began spanking her. At that young age, many of the disciplining issues were for their physical protection, involving warnings regarding dangerous objects like electrical cords, light sockets, and door hinges.

Second, *define the boundaries.* Before we can enforce spanking, we must clarify right and wrong behavior. Our children must understand what the boundaries are and what will happen when those lines are crossed. It would be unfair to spank them for an action that had never been defined as wrong. Thus, we must define what is right and wrong, and forewarn what will happen if they disobey.

Third, *follow through.* Once the rules have been clearly established, they must be enforced when violated. Active, deliberate disobedience is rebellion and must be dealt with. The issue is their will against yours. When your child seeks to assert himself or herself against your will, you must bring about their submission by applying chastisement. They must associate pain with their disobedience.

Remember, the integrity of your word is at stake. If you said you were going to punish disobedience, then when the boundaries have been broken, it must be enforced—or you will break your word.

Consider Susannah Wesley, mother of noted eighteenth-century evangelists John and Charles Wesley, who raised seventeen healthy, active children. Toward the end of her life, her famous son John asked her to put down in writing her philosophy of parenting. As you will see from the following excerpt, her beliefs reflect the traditional understanding of child rearing. This godly woman wrote:

> In order to form the minds of children, the first thing to be done is to conquer the will, and bring them into an obedient temper. To inform the understanding is a work of time, and must with children proceed by slow degrees as they are able to bear it; but the subjecting of the will is a thing which must be done at once, and the sooner the better!
>
> Whenever a child is corrected, it must be conquered; and this will be no hard matter to do, if it be not grown headstrong by too much indulgence. And, if the will of a child is totally subdued, and if it be brought to revere and stand in awe of the parents, then a great

many childish follies and inadvertence may be passed by. Some should be overlooked and taken no notice of, and others mildly reproved. But no willful transgressions ought ever to be forgiven children, without chastisement, more or less as the nature and circumstances of the offense shall require.[3]

Men, we must not only discipline disobedient actions, but defiant attitudes, as well. Defiance comes in many forms—sulking, pouting, whining, temper tantrums, a mean face, back talk, rolling the eyes. All this must be dealt with swiftly because defiance is simply disobedience in the heart that has not yet expressed itself in an action. It is a direct challenge to our parental authority and is a latent form of rebellion.

Fourth, *verbally reprove.* According to Proverbs 29:15, the rod and reproof go hand in hand. We must tell our children why they are getting a spanking, as well as give a rebuke. This requires a restatement of the wrong committed, your personal displeasure in their action or attitude, and a communication that a spanking will be given. This is not a tongue-lashing, nor a heated exchange, but a clear, yet pointed discussion. At this point, we should allow for an appeal if there is some additional information of which we are unaware as to why they have done what they have done. Admittedly, there are times when we do not have the entire story.

Fifth, *spank immediately.* We should not spend a lot of time talking if the occasion calls for a spanking. The longer you put it off, the worse it becomes. A swift punishment is the best policy. Before the child's heart can become harder, and before their guilty conscience can become more seared, chastisement should be quickly administered. If a spanking is the right thing to do, then it is right to do right now.

Be careful to not let the child's confession, tears, or pleadings, no matter how heart-tugging they may be, hold back the discipline. In the Christian life, confession of sin does not eliminate the effects of that sin. King David confessed his sin of adultery and murder, but that did not nullify the painful effects of his sin. Neither should it in your family. If we allow our child's confession of wrongdoing to cancel out the spanking, then he or she will be tempted to make a counterfeit confession simply to avoid a painful spanking.

I can remember once when Grace Anne, who was five years old, deliberately disobeyed us by taking off down the street by herself and leaving our yard. Now, a longstanding rule at our house is that you may never leave the yard without permission. She knew the rule and what the consequences would be. When we found her, thankfully safe, she immediately began to cry, pleading and repeating, "Daddy, I promise I will never do it again. I've learned my lesson. I promise I will obey."

Here was my precious sweet girl, looking up at me pleading with her big brown eyes. It was tempting to just say, "That's okay, sweetheart, just don't do it again." The easy thing would have been to just give her a big hug. But I knew I couldn't—too much was a stake such as her safety, her obedience in the future, and my word. I had to carry out the spanking, which I did despite my reluctance.

Sixth, *inflict pain.* The Old Testament word for "discipline" *(yahsaar)* actually means the infliction of pain causing suffering. Proverbs 23:13–14 says that in applying discipline, fathers should "beat him with the rod." In describing discipline, Hebrews 12:6 uses the word "scourges," which means to take the hide off. All spankings should be painful. A good spanking will last a long time, but a halfhearted spanking may only make the child angry without removing the sin. Make it count!

How many spankings should you give? There is no biblical number, but John MacArthur provides the following as a general rule:[4]

14–18 months	1–2 spankings
19–24 months	1–4 spankings
2–3 years	1–5 spankings
3–4 years	1–6 spankings
4–12 years	1–7 spankings

In administering a spanking, I believe we should *not* use our bare hand. Every verse in Proverbs that mentions spanking speaks about a rod—a neutral object. That way, your child will not associate the pain of the spanking with you personally, but with the instrument used. A rod was a small tree branch or the stem of a bush. In our culture, it might be a small branch, belt, or wooden spoon.

In order to maintain the child's dignity, we should always spank in private. A public spanking would be degrading and humiliating. A good rule is: praise in public, punish in private. If you are in a public place when the wrong occurs, you will want to go to a private place, or wait until you get home. The wait may serve a good purpose by heightening the dread and teaching the lesson.

Also, be in control of yourself. Self-control is what you are trying to teach through your discipline. If you are out of control, it becomes self-defeating. The Bible says, "He who is slow to anger has great understanding, but he who is quick-tempered exalts folly" (Proverbs 14:29).

Seventh, *allow repentance.* After giving the spanking, do not immediately smother your child with hugs and kisses. Not until they confess their wrong, if they have not yet done so. True repentance is never merely sorrow for being caught, but a deep regret for a wrong committed against God and you, and a decision to change.

If there is no expression of repentance, a further discussion will need to ensue. Until there is confession and a change of heart expressed, this is not a settled matter. You may need to step outside the room and let them think about where they are in this matter and what needs to take place. Then return and hopefully bring about the reconciliation and restoration necessary to bring closure to this conflict.

Eighth, *reassure your love.* After giving the spanking and hearing their confession, reassure your love to your child. Physically hold and console them if necessary. Verbally reaffirm your love. I would recommend leaving the room together, not separated, if the matter is resolved. After a spanking, our children took great delight in putting the spanking spoon up with me, bringing a sense of closure in their mind to this episode of discipline.

Also, make sure that you have truly forgiven your child. Don't keep bringing up the offense if this is a settled issue. It should now be put behind you. If it's forgiven, then it should be forgotten.

Ninth, *teach wisdom.* The time immediately after a spanking is always a teachable moment. While the child's heart is sensitive and broken, take advantage of this opportunity to teach God's truth. Show why their actions were wrong and point out the right approach that should have been taken. Many of life's greatest lessons are learned immediately after the storms of adversity. Take the time then to make sure that the truth is well-grounded in their hearts.

Let's review these nine steps in administering a spanking as we bring this chapter to a close. Start early, define the boundaries, follow through, verbally reprove, spank immediately, inflict pain, allow repentance, reassure your love, and teach wisdom.

Dads, this is the legacy of discipline that we must leave with our children. Without it, they will be lacking self-control and be severely handicapped the rest of their lives. But with it, your children will be prepared to successfully live under the God-established authority of those around them.

Does discipline work?

Absolutely.

The Bible says it does. I figure one ounce of what God has to say is worth more than ten tons of what any man has to say. When properly applied, discipline will reroute a child from the wrong path and put him or her onto the road leading to life. "You shall beat them with the rod, and deliver his soul from Sheol" (Proverbs 23:14). That was certainly the case in my own life.

THE BOARD OF EDUCATION

As we bring this chapter on discipline to a conclusion, allow me to share with you from my own life the power of discipline to transform a child's life. When I was a six-year-old little boy, I was having a mid-morning break in kindergarten, sitting at a round table with about six other little boys and girls. A little girl happened to be seated at that table who said something that made everyone else laugh at me. I can't even remember what it was, but I was embarrassed and decided to retaliate.

So, putting my straw into my milk carton, I sucked up all the milk that I could into my mouth and pointed the straw at her. Then, with all the pressure I could muster, I shot the entire mouthful of milk out of the straw, all over her brand-new red sweater. Now, everybody was laughing at *her*.

She ran from the table, locked herself in the bathroom, and would not come out. Needless to say, my action caused quite a commotion in class that day.

When I got home that evening, my father asked me, "Steve, did anything unusual happen at school today?"

"No, sir," I replied.

Posing the question again, my dad repeated, "Are you *sure* nothing unusual happened at school today?" Still not sensing that anything was up, I answered, "No, sir."

Then, with obvious deliberation, my father restated the question, "Steve, are you *absolutely certain* that nothing happened at school today involving a little girl with a red sweater?"

I now had the overwhelming realization that my sin had found me out. Unknown to me, my father had been checking regularly with my school teacher to see how I was doing. Why he felt he needed to monitor my behavior, I'm not sure.

"Yes, sir," I said, "I guess maybe something happened today."

"Steve, because you did wrong at school today *and* because you lied to me," my dad explained, "I'm going to give you a spanking."

My father then proceeded to give me the spanking of my lifetime, which I greatly deserved.

After telling my dad how sorry I was for not being truthful with him, my father lovingly said, "Steve, I have punished you, and you and I are now right. But, ultimately, you have sinned against God, and one day, when you die, God Himself will have to punish you for your sin."

"But Christ has taken your punishment for you," he explained. "That's what the cross is all about. Jesus died for your sins and took your place at the cross. He died in your place and took your punishment for you. If you will believe in Him, He will save you and forgive all your sins."

That sounded like the best news I'd ever heard. Some time later, I prayed to receive Jesus Christ to be my personal Savior and Lord. I can honestly say it was my father's discipline that, as Proverbs says, "delivered my soul from Sheol" and turned my heart toward God, leading me to salvation in Christ.

As I said to begin this chapter, discipline can be, simultaneously, the "best of times and the worst of times." It is a painful experience, but it can also be that which God uses to bring about great blessing. I know this firsthand because I have seen it used that way in my own life to bring me to faith in Christ. And I have seen it happen in the lives of my own children.

Yes, discipline can be the worst of times, but it can also be used to produce the best of times.

For now and for eternity.

CHAPTER 10

WHAT THEY DON'T TEACH YOUR KIDS AT SCHOOL

A Legacy of Wisdom

A MAN BEGINS CUTTING HIS WISDOM TEETH
THE FIRST TIME HE BITES OFF MORE THAN HE CAN CHEW.

—*Herb Caen*

Once there was a wealthy gold miner who had an intelligent son who was destined to take over his business and inherit his fortune. But first, the father sent his son back East to study in the finest engineering school so he could learn about managing the mines.

The young man studied hard and proudly received his degree and diploma. Returning to the mines, he reported to his father, "Dad, I'm ready to go to work. Give me your best mine, and I'll show you how to run it."

The father replied, "No, Son, first you must change into your work clothes and go down into the mine. There you will gain experience. You need to start at the bottom and work your way up."

But the son resisted, "Look, Dad, I've been to school and received my diploma. I know more about mining than you will ever know, all due respects. And if you will just give me your best mine, I will prove it to you."

And so the father, against his better judgment, gave his son the most productive mine he owned. For a while it did well. One day, however, the father received a letter, stating, "Dad, the mine I am working is backed up to the lake. Water is seeping in. We've shored it up, but the shoring does not seem to hold. What do you think we ought to do?"

The father did not answer.

In a few more days, the son wrote again. "Dad, this is serious. We are not able to stop the water. What do you think we ought to do?"

Still no answer from the father.

Finally the son frantically wired his father: IF YOU DO NOT GIVE ME AN ANSWER SOON, WE ARE GOING TO LOSE THE ENTIRE MINE. WHAT SHOULD I DO?

The father wired back: TAKE YOUR DIPLOMA AND SHOVE IT INTO THAT HOLE![1]

Some things are *not* learned in school. While I would never minimize a formal education, there are certain matters no classroom will ever teach you. In a greater sense, there are some issues about life that can only be learned from God. That subject is called wisdom.

It is every father's responsibility to teach his children wisdom. School may give them knowledge, but dads must teach them wisdom. Every father worth his salt desires wisdom for his sons and daughters.

Men, it is important to understand the difference between knowledge and wisdom. Knowledge is *learned;* wisdom is *given.* Knowledge comes by *looking around;* wisdom comes by *looking up.* Knowledge comes by *study;* wisdom comes from *time with God!*

THE VALUE OF WISDOM

Let us turn our attention now to a new facet of Ephesians 6:4—instructing our children in the way of wisdom. The apostle Paul says to us:

Fathers...bring them up in the...instruction of the Lord. (Ephesians 6:4)

"The instruction of the Lord" refers to wisdom—God's wisdom. Earlier in this book, we discovered the subject of wisdom in which we noted that every father must walk in wisdom (Ephesians 5:15). Wisdom is seen as life from God's perspective and knowing how to apply God's truth to each situation that will lead to God's will.

But not only must fathers walk in wisdom, we must also teach wisdom to our children. It is critically important that we be dispensers of godly wisdom to our kids so that they will learn to see life from God's perspective and be able to apply God's truth to each life situation in which they find themselves.

From Ephesians 6:4, we discover how we should teach our children wisdom. By emphasizing three key words in this verse—*fathers, instruction, Lord*—we see that we should instruct our children *personally, biblically, and practically.* Let's consider each of these three now.

DUTY #1:
DADS, TEACH THEM PERSONALLY!
Fathers bring them up in the...
instruction of the Lord.
EPHESIANS 6:4B

From Paul's instruction here, it is clear that God expects fathers to take the lead role in teaching their children. This responsibility cannot be delegated to the church, the school, or anyone else. These may supplement what we are teaching at home, but must never replace it.

Dads, we must teach our kids one on one. Our first ministry must be to our own children. Warren Wiersbe writes, "Home is the place where the children ought to learn about the Lord and the Christian life. It is time that Christian parents stop passing the buck to Sunday School teachers and Christian day-care teachers and start nurturing their children."[2]

In order to do this, we must have close contact with our kids. Intimacy is a prerequisite for the effective imparting of spiritual truth. This requires that we draw close to them and spend quality time with them. The closer, the better.

For example, if I sank 20 putts in a row, you might be impressed with my accuracy. But if I told you that I was only 10 inches away, you would say, "Well, *anyone* can sink putts from that distance." But if you were to move me back to 60 feet, I'm sure to start missing a few putts. That's because distance increases the probability for error. The greater the distance, the greater the probability of error. But the closer we are to the target, the greater our accuracy will be.

CLOSE AND INTIMATE

That's exactly the way it is with fathering. Distance increases error, but closeness increases accuracy. The further we are removed from our children, the greater the chance for missing the mark. The best thing we can do to improve our teaching at home is, quite simply, to draw close to our kids. Getting them on our team goes a long way toward winning the game.

This principle is taught in the book of Proverbs. Solomon said to his child, "Hear, my son, your father's instruction, and do not forsake your mother's teaching" (Proverbs 1:8). It was in the context of closeness to his son that he taught his son spiritual truth. When Solomon says, "Hear, my son," it certainly implies that his words were spoken within hearing distance of his son. Twice more in this particular lesson, he addresses the listener as "My son" (verses 10, 15), underscoring the direct link between father and son. Similarly, we must be directly involved in teaching our children God's wisdom up close and personal.

When our son John was five years old, he received a basketball pole, backboard, goal, and ball for Christmas. It was a regulation size goal, one cemented into the ground, but adjusted down to his size, about five feet high. John had seen his older brothers play basketball all year long, but had never gotten interested until now.

Why was John so excited now to play basketball? Why so interested? The goal was now up close. No longer ten feet tall and unreachable, the shorter goal was now within shooting distance. Closeness to the goal increased his interest and raised his excitement to participate.

That's the way wisdom is to be taught at home. When we are far away and distant, our kids are unexcited. But when we lower ourselves and come down to our kid's level, they become drawn to us and want to learn. We must teach our kid's God's wisdom and that occurs only when we do so up close and personal.

Are *you* personally involved in teaching your children? What are *you* teaching them? Have *you* adopted a hands-on approach to instructing your kids? Are *you* directly participating in their education? Or have *you* delegated your duty to someone else?

Men, be involved *personally*.

DUTY #2:
DADS, TEACH THEM BIBLICALLY!
Fathers bring them up in the...
instruction of the Lord.
EPHESIANS 6:4B

What we teach our children must be anchored in the Word of God. Our instruction must be rooted and grounded in inspired Scripture. All that we impart must flow from the Bible, square with the Bible, and tie back to the Bible.

When Paul says, "Fathers...bring them up...in the instruction of the Lord," this implies that the Word of God must be the core curriculum at home.

From the apostle's own teaching in Ephesians 6, we can surmise that instructing our children involves both the Old and New Testament. After instructing children to obey their parents (verse 1), Paul reinforces this New Testament teaching by quoting two Old Testament passages, Exodus 20:12 and Deuteronomy 5:16 (verses 2–3). This certainly implies that the children in Ephesus had a good working knowledge of the Old Testament as they were being taught New Testament truth.

CHRISTIANITY 101

What does this say to us? We must teach our children the full counsel of God, instructing them in both the Old and New Testaments. We must ground them in both doctrine and duty, impart to them both positional and practical truth, and teach them both God's commands and promises. This requires several things of us:

First, *we must know the Word of God.* Teaching God's wisdom never occurs in a vacuum. You cannot impart what you do not possess. Nor can you teach what you do not know. You cannot give away what you do not grasp. Nor can you take them where you haven't already been.

Every father must love the Lord with all his mind (Matthew 22:37), and this involves training ourselves intellectually to know God's Word. When we cease learning, we cease teaching.

Second, *we must exalt the Son of God.* The "instruction of the Lord" can also mean instruction that is centered in the Lord. Christ is to be the ultimate focus of all we teach at home. Just as all roads lead to Rome, so all our instruction should lead to Christ. All the Scriptures speak of Christ. Consequently, all that we teach our children should point to Him. We must always ask, "What does Jesus say about this subject? What would Jesus do in this situation? What would most glorify Him?

Third, *we must depend upon the Spirit of God.* Men, we can speak truth, but only the Holy Spirit can impart truth. The Bible confirms, "For to us God revealed them through the Spirit; for the Spirit searches all things, even the depth of God" (1 Corinthians 2:10). The Holy Spirit is "the Spirit of truth" who alone can open our children's eyes and instruct their hearts in God's Word. So, we must be consciously dependent upon the Holy Spirit's ministry to take what we teach and apply it to our children's lives.

Men, are *you* growing in your personal knowledge and understanding of the Word of God? Are *you*, in turn, teaching the Word of God to your children? Are *you* teaching out of a deepening well of your own knowledge of Christ?

DUTY #3:
DADS, TEACH THEM PRACTICALLY!
Fathers bring them up in the...
instruction of the Lord.
EPHESIANS 6:4B

It's not enough just to teach biblical truth. We must also apply it in a practical way. The word "instruction" *(nouthesia)* means "putting in mind, to place before the mind." It refers to the verbal instruction that fathers give to their children concerning the practical "how to's" of daily living the will of the Lord.

Commenting on this word "instruction," John MacArthur notes, "This refers to the type of instruction found in the book of Proverbs, where the primary focus is on the training and teaching of children. It does not have as much to do with factual information as with right attitudes and principles of behavior."[3] Likewise, Warren Wiersbe recognizes the connection between "the instruction of the Lord" and the practical instruction of the book of Proverbs when he writes, "In the book of Proverbs, for example, we have an inspired record of a father sharing wise counsel with his son."[4]

With that in mind, let's briefly survey the opening chapters of Proverbs and see the parental instruction that Solomon passed along to his children. Here are fourteen father-son talks, teaching ten essential truths, four being repeated. Dads, these same practical truths must be transferred to our children. If they can grasp these life lessons, they will be prepared to live successfully in whatever God calls them to do. Each of these lessons is an appeal by Solomon to his son to listen carefully to the voice of wisdom. Let's look briefly at these father-son talks and seek to transmit these same truths to our children.

1. ABANDON BAD COMPANY (PROVERBS 1:8–19; 4:10–19)

In this first life lesson, Solomon drives home the truth that our children must be careful with whom they associate. Peer pressure is a strong force. When we go along with others, it can often lead us into trouble. Therefore, Solomon says to his son "Avoid bad company all together." Here is his counsel:

> My son, if sinners entice you, do not consent. If they say, "Come with us, let us lie in wait for blood, let us ambush the innocent without cause; let us swallow them alive like Sheol, even whole, as those who go down to the pit; we shall find all kinds of precious wealth, we shall fill our houses with spoil; throw in your lot with us, we shall all have one purse." My son, do not walk in the way with them. Keep your feet from their path. (Proverbs 1:10–15)

Solomon instructed his son that he must learn to say "no" to other kids who would seek to lure him into trouble. Strength of character is needed to resist the enticement of wrong influences when trouble comes knocking. God says, tell your kids to stay away from them. Saturate their presence with your absence.

My father used to tell me, "Show me what books you read and the company you keep and I'll tell you who you are, or who you will soon become." Fathers, we must instruct our children to choose their friends carefully, and tell them to say "no" when friends attempt to influence them toward wrong behavior.

Again, in another father-son talk, Solomon repeats the same lesson— avoid bad company. By repeating this lesson, he underscores the importance of this truth.

> Do not enter the path of the wicked, and do not proceed in the way of evil men. Avoid it, do not pass by it; turn away from it and pass on. For they cannot sleep unless they do evil; and they are robbed of sleep unless they make someone stumble. For they eat the bread of wickedness, and drink the wine of violence. (Proverbs 4:14–16)

This warning encompasses all kinds of people with whom our children will have contact—classmates, teammates, friends, acquaintances, strangers—those who are portrayed as troublemakers. In fact, these people are so taken up with evil they are unable to sleep until they hurt someone. They are restless to create wickedness and thrive on violence. They feed on trouble as if it were food—they eat it up!

We must counsel our children to stay clear of such people. These other kids are trouble looking for someplace to happen. So instruct your children to pick their friends wisely and advise them not even to hang out with those looking for trouble.

They may need to sit next to someone else in school. Or go to someone else's house. Or stay away from certain places because of who will be there. Consider the following:

First, *affirm their right choices*. With deliberate encouragement, my father used to tell me, "Steve, I'm so pleased with who your friends are." Those affirmations were a powerful motivation to me to keep the right friends. The Bible says, "Do not be deceived: 'Bad company corrupts good morals'" (1 Corinthians 15:33). On the other hand, good company reinforces good morals. So encourage your kids to choose friends with high moral standards.

Then, *teach the value of standing alone*. When Anne and I read Bible stories to our children, we make it a priority to point out "the power of one." When Daniel was in Babylon, he refused to obey the king's law but continued to pray to the God of Israel. Nevertheless, he was willing to stand alone and was willing to suffer the consequences of being thrown into the lion's den (Daniel 6). Elijah also stood alone in the face of the prophets of Baal (1 Kings 18). Always set before your children courageous men and women of God who are willing to stand alone.

Last, *teach them how to say no*. Our kids must learn the power of saying no to their friends. Remind them that just because someone invites them to do something does not mean that they have to do it.

2. OBEY GOD IMMEDIATELY (PROVERBS 1:20–33)

Solomon's next lesson conveyed to his son the truth that God's Word must be obeyed *immediately*. Delayed obedience is no obedience. Our children cannot sow their wild oats today, and then pray for crop failure tomorrow. They will reap what they sow. If they disobey God now, there will be certain consequences that cannot be reversed.

In this second father-son talk, wisdom is personified as a woman standing in the streets and shouting to her children, inviting them to come and follow her. If wisdom's call is refused, tomorrow may be too late to respond. God's Word must be heeded today while there is opportunity.

Wisdom shouts in the street, she lifts her voice in the square; at the head of the noisy streets she cries out; at the entrance of the gates in the city, she utters her sayings: "How long, O naive ones, will you love simplicity? And scoffers delight themselves in scoffing, and fools hate knowledge? Turn to my reproof, behold, I will pour out my spirit on you; I will make my words known to you. Because I called, and you refused; I stretched out my hand, and no one paid attention; and you neglected all my counsel, and did not want my reproof; I will even laugh at your calamity; I will mock when your dread comes, when your dread comes like a storm, and your calamity comes on like a whirlwind, when distress and anguish come on you. Then they will call on me, but I will not answer; they will seek me diligently, but they shall not find me." (Proverbs 1:20–28)

Here wisdom is pictured as someone shouting in the streets, calling out for our attention and vying for our response. The lesson is clear: we must respond to wisdom's call as soon as we hear it, or the day will come, if we refuse wisdom now, it will refuse us when we later call out to wisdom.

How this speaks to our children!

We must teach our kids that they must respond to God's wisdom whenever they hear it. They can never play fast and loose with truth. They must use it or they will lose it. There is always an urgency to respond to God's wisdom the moment it is heard.

Men, our children must obey God now while they are young, before temptations grow stronger. The Bible says, "Remember also your Creator in the days of your youth, before the evil days come" (Ecclesiastes 12:1). If they turn a deaf ear to wisdom now, the day may come when they will finally turn to God, but it will be too late. He will refuse to deliver them from the consequences of their wrong choices.

Every child's heart is either growing softer or harder, but it is never remaining the same. Truth refused hardens the heart. Disobedience makes it more difficult to obey the next time. But truth obeyed today makes obedience easier tomorrow.

Too many fathers have adopted a hands-off approach regarding requiring obedience from their children. Unfortunately, they are content to sit back passively and let their children make up their own mind about the many moral choices before them. But that wasn't Solomon's approach. Neither should it be yours. Are you motivating your children to obey God with a sense of urgency? Are you encouraging first-time obedience as a way of life? Are you affirming your kids when they do obey God promptly?

3. AVOID LOOSE WOMEN (PROVERBS 2:1–22; 5:1–23; 6:20–35; 7:17–27)

This third father-son talk contains the one lesson most repeated by Solomon. This deliberate repetition serves to underscore how important this lesson is. This is one area of a young person's life, that, if not heeded, could ruin the rest of their lives. In these verses, Solomon tells his son, very pointedly, to avoid the adulteress. Through intoxicating flattery, such a seductive woman will attempt to destroy him. Be assured, she is on the prowl, looking for trouble. Look how Solomon represents her:

> (Wisdom will) deliver you from the strange woman, from the adulteress who flatters with her words; that leaves the companion of her youth, and forgets the covenant of her God; for her house sinks down to death, and her tracks lead to the dead; none who go to her return again, nor do they reach the paths of life. (Proverbs 2:16–19)

Dads, we must teach our children that one moment of illicit pleasure will bring a lifetime of destruction. Having ruined her own marriage, this immoral, loose woman will seek to ruin your son's. And it's not just impure women. Young men will attempt to destroy your daughters as well. So get to them before the adulteress does!

Again, Solomon repeats this warning: avoid the seductive woman at all costs. He says:

> For the lips of an adulteress drip honey, and smoother than oil is her

speech; but in the end she is bitter as wormwood, sharp as a two-edged sword. Her feet go down to death, her steps lay hold of Sheol. Keep your way far from her, and do not go near the door of her house. (Proverbs 5:3–5, 8)

This sweet, talking woman—or man—is so deceptive—just like Satan! She comes with pleasant sounding words that are flattering, friendly, flirtatious, but fatal! They are set aflame from hell. Do not get close to her, Solomon warns his sons. Don't go near her apartment or house—stay clear!

Men, we must teach our sons and daughters to stay away from such sweet-talking people of the opposite sex who have no morals, but evil intentions. You tell them, *absence* is the key to abstinence.

As if twice were not enough, Solomon repeats this lesson a third time, again warning his son to avoid the adulteress. Some people say that sexual sin is all right as long as nobody gets hurt. But God's Word says somebody *always* gets hurt. Listen to Solomon's advice:

For the commandment is a lamp, and the teaching is light; and reproofs for discipline are the way of life, to keep you from the evil woman, from the smooth tongue of the adulteress. Do not desire her beauty in your heart, nor let her catch you with her eyelids. (Proverbs 6:23–25)

What Solomon said so many years ago is just as relevant today. It is no different. There are certain women who are sexually promiscuous that will destroy your sons if they can. So, we must counsel our children to watch over their hearts, guard their eyes, and look away from her.

A fourth time, Solomon repeats this simple truth—stay as far away from loose women as you possibly can.

And behold, a woman comes to meet him, dressed as a harlot and cunning of heart. She is boisterous and rebellious; her feet do not remain at home; she is now in the streets, now in the squares, and lurks by every corner. So she seizes him and kisses him, and with a brazen face she says to him: "I was due to offer peace offerings; today

I have paid my vows. Therefore, I have come out to meet you, to seek your presence earnestly, and I have found you."... Now therefore my son listen to me, and pay attention to the words of my mouth. Do not let your heart turn aside to her ways, do not stray into her paths. (Proverbs 7:10–15, 24–25)

Our sons are no match for the enticing ploys of this woman who is dressed to kill—literally. As the song says, "she's a devil with a blue dress on." She's always on the prowl, looking for her next prey. So cunning is she that she will even come to church (Notice, she says, "I was due to offer peace offerings") to hunt for her next catch.

This lesson must be taught to our daughters as well. Sad to say, there are young men, driven by their hormones, who are on the search for our daughters and will destroy your home in one moment of illicit pleasure. Men, we must protect our sons and daughters. What can we do?

First, *teach them sex education.* At the appropriate time, teach your children what they need to know about "the birds and the bees." Rather than letting them learn from the crude talk of classmates, let them learn it from you, as you explain sex from a biblical perspective. There are many valuable resources at your Christian bookstore that will be of great help.

Second, *monitor their dates and activities.* I can assure you when the first guy comes to our house to see Grace Anne, he will be checked out by the FBI, the CIA, and the Secret Service. He'll have to walk through a metal detector to get into our living room. Don't let your kids go out with just anyone. Make it the law to only date Christians of high morals.

Third, *elevate the virtue of virginity.* Many parents today are participating in a public ceremony with their children, where their children commit before God that they will keep their chastity until marriage.

Fourth, *keep them busy in wholesome activities.* Many kids fall into trouble because they have nothing better to do with their time. One reason I like our children to participate in sports is because, among other reasons, they don't have much free time to get into trouble. Encourage your kids to find a wholesome extra-curricular activity. Do fun things together as a family. Promote excellence in their academics. If they will pursue these things, they will not have time left for trouble.

4. TRUST GOD'S SOVEREIGNTY (PROVERBS 3:1–12)

The next lesson Solomon taught his son was to trust God completely. He urges his child to put God first and obey Him, no matter what, and to submit to His Word, fear Him, and honor Him with your wealth. Listen to Solomon's fatherly advice:

> Trust in the Lord with all your heart, and do not lean on your own understanding. In all your ways acknowledge Him, and He will make your paths straight. Do not be wise in your own eyes; fear the Lord and turn away from evil. It will be healing to your body, and refreshment to your bones. Honor the Lord from your wealth, and from the first of all your produce; so your barns will be filled with plenty, and your vats will overflow with new wine. (Proverbs 3:5–10)

To trust God means to lean fully upon the Lord in every situation, and not relying upon your own wisdom or solutions. "Heart" refers to all that you are on the inside—one's emotions, intellect, understanding, discernment, reflections, and will. With our entire inner man, we must trust Him completely. No matter what obstacle or opposition stands before us, we must teach our children to trust God explicitly, believing that He will remove all that prevents us from doing God's will.

This life lesson applies across the board to every area of a kid's life, just like it does to an adult's. Whenever they have an important decision to make, they must be persuaded that God knows what is best. He can be trusted completely to lead perfectly in every choice they make.

Needless to say, our children need to see us put our trust in God in every situation of life. As they observe us walking with God, they will be encouraged to do the same. Let's face it, faith is contagious—especially at home! Our trust in God will encourage theirs.

5. ACT WITH INTEGRITY (PROVERBS 3:13–35)

The fifth lesson in which Solomon instructed his son deals with guarding one's integrity and maintaining principle. Solomon said:

> Do not withhold good from those to whom it is due, when it is in your power to do it. Do not say to your neighbor, "Go, and come

back, and tomorrow I will give it," when you have it with you. Do not devise harm against your neighbor, while he lives in security beside you. Do not contend with a man without cause, if he has done you no harm. Do not envy a man of violence, and do not choose any of his ways. For the crooked man is an abomination to the Lord; but He is intimate with the upright. (Proverbs 3:27–32)

Solomon taught his son about integrity in relationships. Each of these five maxims begins with the words "Do not." Here are five negatives that help define integrity.

Teach your children if they owe someone money, they should pay their debt. Always pay your bills on time. And as you come across people in need, be generous and help them as you can.

Do everything possible to live at peace with others. Don't cause trouble for those around you. Learn to get along with other people. Never seek personal gain at the expense of someone else. Such profit is loss.

Children should not make a hero out of someone who, although successful by the world's standards, is unprincipled. God is with the one who is upright. Better is little if God is in it than much gain without the Lord.

Do not withhold paying wages to a hired laborer. (verses 27–28)
Do not plot harm against another who has done you no wrong. (verses 29–30)
Do not envy an ungodly man, no matter how much money he has. (verse 31–32)

6. Acquire God's Wisdom (Proverbs 4:1–9)

In this next lesson, Solomon taught his son to acquire much wisdom, as much as he can. He compares wisdom to a precious commodity that is to be valued above all else. Whatever it costs you, buy it up!

When I was a son to my father, tender and the only son in the sight of my mother. Then he taught me and said to me, "let your heart hold fast my words. Acquire wisdom! Acquire understanding! Do not forget, nor turn away from the words of my mouth. Do not forsake her, and she will guard you; love her, and she will watch over you. The beginning of wisdom is: Acquire wisdom; and with all your acquiring, get understanding." (Proverbs 4:3–7)

Just as David taught Solomon God's wisdom as a child, so Solomon is now committed to teaching his sons the same. We must do the same. One of the greatest responsibilities of parents is to encourage their children to become wise. Fathers must urge their children to turn to God for wisdom.

Men, we must influence our children to buy up wisdom like a precious commodity. If they want wisdom, they must decide to go after it. It takes resolved determination on their part to search the Scriptures and to seek the Lord in prayer in order to attain it.

Encourage your kids to read and study the Word of God, which is able to make them wise (2 Timothy 3:15). Call them to walk in close fellowship with Christ, in whom are hidden all the treasures of wisdom and understanding (Colossians 2:3). Teach them to pray earnestly, from which comes wisdom from above (James 1:5).

7. KEEP YOUR HEART ALERT (PROVERBS 4:20–27)

The seventh lesson of wisdom that Solomon passed on to his son is: watch over your heart carefully. The heart must be closely guarded and carefully monitored. He says:

> Watch over your heart with all diligence, for from it flow the springs of life. Put away from you a deceitful mouth, and put devious lips far from you. Let your eyes look directly ahead, and let your gaze be fixed straight in front of you. Watch the path of your feet, and all your ways will be established. Do not turn to the right nor to the left; turn your foot from evil. (Proverbs 4:23–27)

The word "heart" refers to our entire inner being—our mind, emotions, and will. A child's entire life flows out of the inner well of their heart. If they will watch over their heart, they will channel the direction of their life. Consequently, we must be constantly emphasizing to our children the necessity of a pure heart. They may be tempted to look on the outward appearance—such as designer labels, name brands, car makes—but God looks on their heart (1 Samuel 16:7). In a day when the world is causing our children to be concerned with externals, we must be emphasizing their heart.

8. ABSTAIN FROM EXCESSIVE DEBT (PROVERBS 6:1–5)

The eighth lesson that Solomon teaches his son is a warning against foolish financial arrangements. Many a young person has overextended himself financially and acted irresponsibly.

> My son, if you have become surety for your neighbor, have given a pledge for a stranger, if you have been snared with the words of your mouth, have been caught with the words of your mouth, do this then, my son, and deliver yourself; if you have come into the hand of your neighbor, go humble yourself, and importune your neighbor. (Proverbs 6:1–3)

This warning is not against borrowing or lending per se, but against being held accountable for another person's high-interest loan. Becoming surety means to cosign a note for someone that involves paying an exorbitant interest rate for another person's loan. If your children find themselves in such a situation, instruct them to get out of it as soon as they can. Helping someone in need is one thing, but exposing yourself to a risk by making an unconditional pledge to underwrite someone else's debt is foolish. The warning here is not against borrowing or lending, but against being personally responsible for someone else's higher interest loan.

A person ensnared by a foolish debt agreement should, like a trapped animal, struggle frantically to become free of it. One should free himself from such a debt agreement, even it requires self-humiliation and relentless pleading.

Men, we must teach our children to become good managers of their money. We must counsel them to avoid entering into any financial agreement that assumes someone else's debt, whether their own or another's. Instruct them to use great discretion in assuming personal debt such as a car loan, a college education loan, a credit card, a charge account, or store credit. Indebtedness must be approached with extreme caution, care and concern.

9. ASSUME HARD WORK (PROVERBS 6:6–11)

The ninth lesson Solomon teaches his son is the value of hard work. Laziness is a sin that dishonors God and must be avoided. He challenges his son to be an industrious worker.

> Go to the ant, O sluggard, observe her ways and be wise, which, having no chief, officer or ruler, prepares her food in the summer, and gathers her provision in the harvest. How long will you lie down, O sluggard? When will you arise from your sleep? A little sleep, a little slumber, a little folding of the hands to rest and your poverty will come in like a vagabond, and your need like an armed man. (Proverbs 6:6–11)

Every father must guard against allowing his children to become "sluggards." A sluggard is a lazy, irresponsible person lacking direction, drive, and desire. Too many parents today have so spoiled their children that they have become passive, lethargic, and slack. Instead, they should learn from the industrious ant who is self-initiating in its work. The enterprising ant anticipates future needs, storing food in the summer before winter comes. In the same way, a wise son or daughter will learn to work hard today without procrastinating or waiting for others to do his or her work for them. Children who work only when forced to do not possess wisdom.

Dads, give your children work assignments at home. Encourage them to save their money and plan ahead for the future. Require a reasonable amount of help around the house.

10. MAINTAIN HARMONY AND PEACE (PROVERBS 6:12–19)

The tenth lesson Solomon taught his son is a final call to live in harmony and peace with others. He tells his son to avoid stirring up strife and discord with others. Here's what he said:

> A worthless person, a wicked man, is the one who walks with a false mouth, who winks with his eyes, who signals with his feet, who points with his fingers; who with perversity in his heart devises evil continually, who spreads strife. Therefore his calamity will come

suddenly; instantly he will be broken, and there will be no healing. There are six things which the Lord hates, yes seven which are an abomination to Him: haughty eyes, a lying tongue, and hands that shed innocent blood, a heart that devises wicked plans, feet that run rapidly to evil, a false witness who utters lies, and one who spreads strife among brothers. (Proverbs 6:12–19)

Solomon refers to the person who can cause discord by merely signaling his friends to join him in trouble. Such a one plans dissension when other unsuspecting people are totally unaware. A troublemaker stirs up discord with haughty eyes, a lying tongue, murderous hands, a wicked heart, and evil feet—all this causing strife in the family or among friends. By destroying others, they destroy their own lives.

Similarly, every father must teach his children to learn how to get along with other people. This lesson begins at home. If they cannot get along with their siblings, they will learn the art of arguing and disunity at a young age. We must correct them when they cause trouble, provoke others, or give a haughty look. Such sins must be dealt with swiftly.

Men, these are the ten lessons that Solomon taught his sons and must be the curriculum of our teaching at home as well. These are timeless truths for successful living. They worked in Solomon's day, and they will work today. But they will only work when we teach them diligently. We must teach them again and again. Repetition is still a great teacher. Like driving a nail into a hard board, it takes many hits with the hammer, over and over and over again, before it is driven into the board. We must drive these truths home over and over again with our children.

Schools may help them make a living, but only wisdom can help them make a life.

WORK IS "NOT" A FOUR-LETTER WORD

A Legacy of Responsibility

THE BEST INHERITANCE A PARENT CAN LEAVE A CHILD IS A WILL TO WORK.

—*Hippocrates*

Every March, we set aside a family workday which is a spring cleaning for the yard. Everybody in the family pitches in together and helps get the yard back in shape after a long winter. This was particularly true a few years ago when we moved into a house with a yard that had been severely neglected for some time.

All six of us—Anne, the four kids, and I—attacked the yard with a vengeance, sawing off dead limbs, pruning back shrubs, edging the sidewalk, weeding the flower beds, mowing the yard, cleaning out the gutters—the works! We looked like an ant colony scurrying about. Andrew and James were actually fighting over who would get to saw off the next limb. And Grace Anne and John were dragging the cut-off limbs out to the street.

As the day wore on, I suddenly remembered that an NCAA basketball tournament game was about to come on. So when no one was looking, I sneaked inside the house to get a drink of water—and *just happened* to turn on the television in time for tip-off.

Before I knew it, it was half time, and I had people—Andrew and James—looking for me and, once finding me, reclining on the sofa with me, watching the game.

Soon, with perspiration beading down her forehead and dirt smeared on her cheeks, Anne came dragging through the house like a wandering sheep dog looking for her lost flock. When I looked up and saw her, I suddenly remembered that I had completely forgotten to get that drink of water.

Instantly, Anne gave me "the look." Guys, you know exactly what I'm talking about. Eye contact that could freeze water in the Sahara desert.

"Where have *you* been?" she quizzed.

With that indicting question, I realized that I had gotten sidetracked in the midst of our family workday and had lured our boys to do the same. I had been a bad influence on my boys, causing them to stop their work to join me on my "extended" break. In an attempt to get us back on track, I clicked off the television and told Andrew and James that we'd better get back outside to cut off some more limbs—knowing that I had just climbed out on a shaky one myself.

HARD WORK PAYS OFF

As fathers, we all need to teach our children the value of hard work. Rather than trying to get out of work, we need to be passing on a legacy of responsibility. In a day in which work has become a four-letter word, we need to teach our children that working hard is a virtue to be pursued, not a curse to be avoided. And it's not enough just to dictate that our kids work. We must also work alongside them and model before them the value of hard work.

Someone once asked a general in the Israeli army why their soldiers are so outstanding. The general replied, "It's because our generals do not send our troops into battle, we lead them."

That's exactly how we must lead our families. As the head of our homes, we are not to be sitting in an ivory tower, barking orders for our troops to follow. Instead, we must get down in the trenches with them and be personally involved as we work alongside them. Our children will never know the value of hard work unless they see it at home demonstrated in us as dads.

But let's face it, we live in a culture that has a very skewed work ethic. We've all seen those deeply meaningful license plate frames that have such profound philosophies as:

◆ "I'd rather be *fishing.*"
◆ "I'd rather be *flying.*"

♦ "I'd rather be *golfing*."
♦ "I'd rather be *skiing*."
♦ "I'd rather be *sailing*."
♦ "I'd rather be *biking*."
♦ "I'd rather be *4-wheeling*."

In other words, *anything* but work. *Whatever* I'm doing has no value compared to playing. To many people, work simply finances their pleasures. Maybe you've seen the bumper sticker that says, "I owe, I owe, so off to work I go." Such a worldly philosophy views work primarily as a way to pay off one's debts, or to fund one's lifestyle.

I saw another bumper sticker that says, "He who dies with the most toys wins." This mentality conveys the basic belief that people would rather play than work. Another bumper sticker says, "Work fascinates me—I can sit and watch it for hours." The message is the same. "Hard work may not kill me—but why take the chance?"

Funny on the surface, these sayings reflect a deep illness in America today which depreciates the value of old-fashioned, hard work.

I'm waiting to see a bumper sticker on the back of a golf cart that says, "I'd Rather Be Working." Or, a license tag that says, "Thank God its Monday." We really have a warped view of work today, but honestly, that isn't anything new. Even in the days of the apostle Paul, there was need for clear teaching on the high value of work.

Why is work good? Why is there a high calling to our work? Because work is something that God has purposed for our good. There is intrinsic value to work. Listen to what the apostle Paul says:

> Slaves, be obedient to those who are your masters according to the flesh, with fear and trembling, in the sincerity of your heart, as to Christ; not by way of eye service as men-pleasers, but as slaves of Christ, doing the will of God from the heart. With good will render service, as to the Lord, and not to men. (Ephesians 6:5–7)

Although addressed to all believers, this passage contains truth that all fathers must pass on to their children. Because these verses immediately follow the central New Testament verse on parenting—Ephesians 6:4—they have special significance for fathers. If we are to teach our kids "the instruction of the Lord," then those verses which immediately follow such an admonition must be included. If anything would be considered "the instruction of the Lord," it must be these verses.

According to this passage, work is a part of the will of God for our lives. Because it is a calling from Christ, our work is to be carried out as to the Lord just like any other spiritual discipline. Let's consider now what the Scripture has to say about work and how it relates to our fathering.

PERSPECTIVE #1:
DADS, TEACH WORK'S VALUE!

Be obedient to those who are your masters
according to the flesh, with fear and trembling,
in the sincerity of your heart, as to Christ.

EPHESIANS 6:5

In the very beginning, God created man so that he might serve Him and glorify His name on the earth. In part, that's what it means to be created in the image of God (Genesis 1:26–28). Within this context, the image of God refers to our God-given capacity to work and rule over God's work. God Himself worked six days in creating the world and then rested on the seventh. On the sixth day, He created man in His image. Consequently, we are like God when we work.

Unfortunately though, some people assume that work is a curse, the result of Adam's sin. But the truth is, work *preceded* the Fall. Adam's original sin and God's subsequent curse upon His creation meant that man would labor by the sweat of his brow (Genesis 3:19), but work itself is intrinsically good. Solomon understood this high calling of work when he wrote:

There is nothing better for a man than to eat and drink and tell himself that his labor is good. This also I have seen, that it is from the hand of God. For who can eat and who can have enjoyment without Him? (Ecclesiastes 2:24–25)

Rightly does Solomon view one's work as a gift from God. Without God, nothing satisfies. But as our lives are lived in close fellowship with Him, everything—including our work—takes on great meaning. Again, Solomon writes:

> I know that there is nothing better for them than to rejoice and to do good in one's lifetime; moreover, that every man who eats and drinks sees good in all his labor—it is the gift of God. (Ecclesiastes 3:12–13)

In other words, we should cheerfully accept work as from God Himself and see great good in performing it. Do your best, Solomon says, in all your labor and receive from it great pleasure and satisfaction. Moreover, Solomon says:

> Furthermore, as for every man to whom God has given riches and wealth, He has also empowered him to eat from them and to receive his reward and rejoice in his labor, this is the gift of God. (Ecclesiastes 5:19)

Again, work is to be seen as a gift from God. Not a substandard activity to be endured. But a gift—even a calling from God—to be enjoyed with personal satisfaction for a job well done.

As we come to the New Testament, Paul says the same. Our work is to be done "as to the Lord." If we see our job as merely serving our employer, then we will only work for temporal reward. But work is a high calling from God, and should motivate us to work for eternal reward.

Work is not just a way to pay bills. It is a way to serve God. It is an expression of worship rendered unto the Lord. We are to do all that we do to the glory of God (1 Corinthians 10:31), including our work. Ultimately, God is my Boss, the One for whom I work. He's the One who hired me, the One who evaluates me, the One who promotes me, and the One who pays me. "All things are from Him and through Him and to Him" (Romans 11:36).

Expanding upon this truth, Paul says that work is "doing the will of God" (Ephesians 6:6). Work is a part of the perfect will of God for our children's lives, depending upon their age. His divine will which is "good and acceptable and perfect" (Romans 12:2) includes their work.

In addition, Paul says that our work is to be "as to the Lord, and not to men." We don't work for men, but for the God who calls us to perform a particular task. Therefore, our work is noble and has eternal value. It is elevated above the ordinary and it, therefore, is transcendent because it comes from God and is to be rendered to God. No matter how mundane any job may seem, whether it is changing the oil or changing diapers, there is dignity and virtue attached to it if God calls us to do it as a part of His will.

A God-Glorifying Work Ethic

A construction foreman approached one of his workers who was busy laying bricks at the foundation of a new church. The foreman asked, "What are you doing?"

"Can't you see? I'm laying bricks," he replied.

The foreman then proceeded to another bricklayer and asked, "What are you doing?"

"I'm building a church," the second laborer said.

The foreman then walked over to a third bricklayer and asked the same question, "What are you doing?"

But this man had a totally different perspective. He answered, "I'm building a house of worship for the glory of God."

All three were doing the same work. But the first two were occupied only with the task. The third man saw the big picture. He worked to serve God.

So, how do we teach this transcendent view of work to our children? How do we instill this virtue within them?

First, *teach them God's perspective on work.* Every job is an opportunity to serve Him and, as such, should be entered into with passion to glorify Him. Our work matters to God. There should be dignity and virtue attached to it, no matter how small or insignificant the task may seem.

For example, I recently had to sit down with my twin boys and talk to them about their grades. I felt that they were more capable than the scores they were bringing home. I shared with them, "Whether then you eat or drink or whatever you do, do all to the glory of God" (1 Corinthians 10:31). "Every activity in life," I explained to them, "is to be done with a commitment to excellence that will glorify God, even your school assignments." Anything less than the best is sin. So, teach your children that work is a noble virtue.

Second, *model for them the value of hard work*. The attitudes that we model in front of our children toward our work will have a powerful effect upon them. We elevate work in their eyes when we carry it out faithfully, wholeheartedly, and with a good spirit. But to the contrary, when we come home grumbling about our boss, or complaining about a client, we tarnish the eternal virtue of work before their impressionable eyes.

Also, we should be faithful and diligent in our own attendance at work. When we call in sick in order to go hunting with our kids, what are we telling them about the nobility of work?

Third, *give your children work assignments at home*. Depending upon the ages of your children, every family member should have responsibilities at home. In years past, these work assignments were called "chores." Today, the same should be required of our children as it serves a useful purpose in building his or her character. A child should never grow up thinking that everything revolves around him. Yet, we reinforce irresponsibility when we fail to give them a part of the load at home to carry—such as making their beds, cleaning their rooms, vacuuming, dusting, setting and cleaning the dinner table, washing dishes, taking out the trash, and mowing the lawn.

Fourth, *work on a project together with them*. There once was a time when America was an agricultural and industrial society and children worked alongside their dad daily. If they grew up on the farm, children worked in the field throughout the day. When the child married, they often would stay on the family farm, build a home on the property, and continue to work with dad. And when dad died, they took over the farm and did the same work with their own children.

But no more. Nowadays, we play with our children, but rarely work with them. This neglect needs to be reversed. As dads, we should take on a work project together with our children. It will be a bonding experience with our kids that will knit our hearts together.

What can you do to work together? Start a business together—be it a lawn mowing service, a lemonade stand, or a paper route. Do a school assignment together—like a science project or a history report. Serve an elderly couple in the church together—rake their yard, repair their roof, paint the garage.

PERSPECTIVE #2:
DADS, TEACH WORK'S VIRTUE!

Be obedient to those who are your masters
according to the flesh, with fear and trembling,
in the sincerity of your heart, as to Christ;
not by way of eye service, as men-pleasers,
but as slaves of Christ, doing the will of God
from the heart. With good will render service,
as to the Lord, and not to men.

EPHESIANS 6:5–7

As fathers, we must concern ourselves, not only with teaching the *value* of work, but also with imparting the *virtues* of work. It's not just *what* we do that's important, but *how* we do it. Let's turn our attention now to the character with which work must be carried out.

Character, it has been said, is what you are in secret when no one sees you. Reputation is what others think about you, but character is what God knows about you. So, what character qualities should be instilled in our children regarding their work responsibilities? As we look at Ephesians 6:5–7, let me point out six timeless truths that should mark the way our children learn to do their work.

1. WORK TEACHES HUMILITY

Paul addressed these early Christian workers as "slaves" (verse 5). In the first century, the Roman Empire was served by millions of servants who were, for the most part, treated like animals and equipment by their masters. In fact, they were owned by their masters and subject to their every command and whim. In Bible times, there were two working classes: there were slaves and masters, and virtually no middle class. There were the haves and the have-nots. Today, we would call these two groups employees and employers.

These slaves existed to serve others, never themselves. They were always considering the interests of others as more important than their own. These slaves lived to support others, not themselves.

That's how most workers in the marketplace today see themselves. Instead, the average worker concerns himself with being the primary beneficiary of his labor. But, no matter whether you work for someone else, or whether you are self-employed, or whether others work for you, we are all called to serve others. Either we serve the public, or we serve the company, or we serve the customer, or we serve a client, or we serve our boss. Everyone who works, in one way or another, works for someone else. We are all in the business of serving others. We must get that across to our children.

As the apostle Paul summarized his approach to life, he said, "Let a man regard us in this manner as servants of Christ, and stewards of the mysteries of God" (1 Corinthians 4:1). A servant *(hupereites)* was a third-level gallery slave who pulled an oar in a sea-faring ship. And you know what a steward is, don't you? Every time I fly, a stewardess or steward serves me a coke or coffee. They exist to attend to the need of others.

That's the approach toward work that we must instill within our children. Unfortunately, this attitude of humility is gone today, especially among young people. Nobody wants to be the servant; everyone wants to be served. In a generation of self-seeking consumers, we are cutting against the grain to mold our children into the image of humility and servanthood. But we must, if they are to be like Christ.

Sometimes I'll ask one of my children to pick up the mess in the bathroom. There will be several piles of clothes dumped all over the floor. Towels will be strewn everywhere. Tennis shoes scattered in piles along with belts, jackets, pants, socks, shirts, and sweaters stacked to the ceiling.

The inevitable response is, "But, Dad I didn't do all this. Why should I pick up someone else's clothes?"

"Because that's what a servant does," I will answer. "He does work for other people. He doesn't just pick up his own clothes, but everyone else's too. A servant exists for others, not for himself."

2. WORK TEACHES OBEDIENCE

A slave exists to do whatever he's told to do. Paul says, "Slaves, be obedient to those who are your masters according to the flesh" (verse 5). A slave wouldn't think of resisting his master, nor doing his own thing.

Children are to carry out their assignments in just the same way. In whatever arena of life they find themselves, they are to obey those over them, whether it be a boss, a parent, a policeman, a teacher, a coach, or a scout master. They must carry out their orders as the Nike ads say, "Just do it."

However, all too often, when our children are asked to do something, it launches a series of high-powered negotiations, replete with counterproposal, rebuttal, and another counterproposal. Then plea bargaining ensues as if they are card-carrying union members.

When our children were very young we implemented what we call the "first time obey" rule. We explained that they were to obey the first time we asked them to do something—not the second, third, or fourth time. In the long run, when consistently carried out, this saves a lot of negotiating and questioning.

3. WORK TEACHES RESPECT

Slaves are to serve "with fear and trembling" (verse 5). An attitude of respect for superiors over us should always characterize the spirit of our work. The honor due parents (Ephesians 6:2) should overflow to bosses. The best politics at work is to do a good job with a great attitude. In the long run, such respect will get you further along with the powers-that-be than anything else you can do. Even if an employer is demanding and difficult to work for, we still owe him respect because it is actually God whom we serve.

Men, we must teach this kind of respect to our children as they approach their work assignments, whether in the home toward you or out of the house toward others. Bad attitudes cannot be tolerated when they approach their work. They must carry out their chores with godly fear toward God.

4. WORK TEACHES SINCERITY

As our children work, they must do so with "sincerity of...heart" (verse 5). In other words, what they do, should be done without complaining, bickering, or criticizing as though God were always watching, which He is.

I can still hear my father's words ringing in my ear, "Any job worth doing is a job worth doing well." That should always be our approach to work, and that must be taught to our children. Any job, no matter how menial it may seem, should always be approached with sincerity of heart—whether it's taking out the trash, picking up the room, or washing the dishes.

The other night, one of my sons said, "Dad, can I listen to classical music while I do my homework?" I said, "Yes, you may, but only classical music."

As soon as I said that, I had a feeling that that would be too great a temptation for him. Sure enough it was, because I soon heard through the wall something else. (It wasn't all that bad. In fact, it turned out to be a Winston Churchill speech.) But, he had no idea that I could hear the sound through the walls.

I walked upstairs to remind him of what boundaries I had established. After reprimanding him, I said, "Buddy, you may not think that I can hear, but I usually can. But remember this—God can always hear. Know that he's always watching and listening."

That heavenly mind set produces great sincerity of heart and causes our children not to be men-pleasers, or father-pleasers, but God-pleasers. If you please God, it doesn't matter whom you displease. And if you displease God, it doesn't matter whom you please.

5. WORK TEACHES WHOLEHEARTEDNESS

Our children should never do no less than what is expected of them, and if anything, they should exceed the standard. Paul says that we are to work "not by way of eye service, as men-pleasers, but as slaves of Christ" (verse 6). In other words, our kids must not be motivated to work only when others are watching us. Such laziness comes from halfheartedness and reflects a sub-standard motivation. Because they are "slaves of Christ" they must always work hard and always do their best before God.

Cathy Rigby was a member of the U.S. Women's Gymnastics Team in the 1972 Olympics at Munich. She had only one goal in mind—to win a gold medal.

For many years, she trained hard to reach her goal.

On the day she was scheduled to perform, she prayed for the strength and the control to get through her routine without making any mistakes. She was focused and tense with determination not to let herself or her country down.

Cathy performed well, but when it was all over and the winners were announced, her name was not among them.

She was crushed. Soon afterward, Cathy joined her parents in the stands all set for a good cry. As she sat down she could barely manage to say, "I'm sorry. I did my best."

"I know that you know that," her dad said, "and I'm sure God knows that, too."

Then, Cathy recalls, her dad said ten words that she has never forgotten, "*Doing* your best is more important than being the best."

Gentlemen, we must impress upon our children always to do their very best in whatever they do. More important than what they do is how they do it.

6. WORK TEACHES SELF-INITIATION

In addition, Paul says that it must be done "with good will" (verse 7). This word *(evonoia)* means to work with an eager attitude that does not need external prompting or compelling. It means to be self-motivated with enthusiasm and zeal that thrusts one into an endeavor. This is what we must cultivate in our children. They must always be self-motivated to tackle whatever assignment is given to them. This begins early by being diligent to clean up their room, take out the trash, and do their homework and household chores by their own motivation. They must be just as motivated for work as they are for pleasure.

For instance, I've noticed sometimes with my own children that to wake up on Monday morning is like raising the dead. I walk into their bedroom and raise their blinds, pull off their covers, tickle their rib cage, turn on the lights, and, after all that, still feel compelled to shout, "Lazarus, come forth."

By contrast, if we are going to go play golf on Saturday morning, I can't even tiptoe down the hallway to approach their bedroom without them throwing off their covers, jumping out of bed, popping to their feet, and throwing on their clothes—all without me having to whisper one word. Strange.

What a difference self-motivation makes. The challenge for us as fathers is to teach our children to have that same "good will" toward their work as they have toward their play.

Coach Tom Landry, one-time coach of the World Champion Dallas Cowboys, said, "The job of a coach is to make men do what they don't want to do, in order to be what they've always wanted to be."[1]

Men, that's exactly what God calls us to do with our children. We need to be like coaches lighting a fire under them in order to help them be what God wants them to be.

In other words, we must encourage our children to be motivated on their own to fulfill the obligations before them and not to wait until dad or mom has to apply pressure to get started. The child who must wait for his or her parents motivation to start and finish a task is the child who will be emotionally paralyzed and dysfunctional as an adult.

This is how every child must be taught to carry out his or her work. If these character qualities can be instilled in our children, then they will be positioned to be successful in life, no matter what God calls them to do.

PERSPECTIVE #3:
DADS, TEACH WORK'S VICTORY!

Knowing that whatever good thing each one does,
this he will receive back from the Lord, whether
slave or free. And masters, do the same things to them,
and give up threatening, knowing that both their
Master and yours is in heaven, and there is
no partiality with Him.

EPHESIANS 6:8–9

As fathers, we must be constantly pointing out to our children the great reward of a job well done. When their work is done in a way that glorifies God, their life will be greatly blessed. As Paul brings this section on work ethics to a conclusion, he writes saying, whether or not our work is recognized or appreciated by others, God always takes note and will faithfully reward us. That's what we must always be instilling into our children—a deep God-consciousness that causes them to seek His favor, not men's.

We live in a world marked by inequity and unfairness. The one who works hard may, unfortunately, be overlooked by his employer for a raise, a promotion, or proper recompense. The race does not always go to the swift. The reward does not always go to the most deserving.

In light of such inequities, we must remind our children that God knows and God rewards. No job that is done in His name and for His glory will pass His notice or fail to receive His blessing.

For a job well done, we can say that God's reward comes on two different dimensions—*now and future.* Presently, hard work brings the reward of proven character in the lives of our children. Character qualifiers like faithfulness, humility, and integrity are built into them when they work hard, whether or not they are recognized by their boss. No price tag can be put on such a reward. Likewise, there is the present reward of financial renumeration (1 Timothy 5:18), personal satisfaction (Ecclesiastes 5:20), and often personal recognition.

There is also the future aspect of reward from our labor. One day, we will all stand before God—our children included—and we will be scrutinized and evaluated by Him concerning, among many things, our work. No part of our lives will escape His all-seeing gaze. If we will fulfill His vocational call upon our lives with faithfulness, then a great reward from God awaits us and our children.

This is the eternal perspective that we want to instill in our children. Our work matters to God. Right now counts forever. "Whatever you do, do your work heartedly; as for the Lord rather than for men; knowing that from the Lord you will receive the reward of the inheritance. It is the Lord Christ whom you serve" (Colossians 3:23–24).

The highest motivation should always be to please the Lord. Whether or not a parent, a teacher, an employer, or a coach recognizes our children for a job well done, they should have the satisfaction of knowing that they have pleased God whether or not they are recognized by men.

A LIFE LESSON

This past summer, our family experienced a very vivid illustration of this very truth. Though painful at the time, it served to remind us that our reward comes from God, not men.

Our two oldest boys, Andrew and James, played on the Junior Golf tour in the area where we live. Because they have some special talent to play the game, I decided to "play them up" in the next older age bracket. I was told that stiffer competition would make them better golfers.

However, after two weeks of playing with the older boys, I realized that this had been a tragic mistake. The language that spewed from many of these boys on the Junior Tour was obscene. I had to make a tough decision, but one that I knew was right. Three weeks into the tour's schedule, I took my boys out of the older division and put them back down with their own age group.

Fortunately, the language was cleaned up—and both James and Andrew competed well with each boy winning tournaments. James also finished second and third in most of the other tournaments, and although he missed getting in on the beginning of the season, he accumulated enough points to finish second on the tour for the entire year.

At the end of the summer, there was a very nice awards banquet for the

Junior golfers and their parents at a local country club in which the kids would be recognized by age groups for first, second, and third. By common consensus, all the boys had tallied up their points and knew that James had come in second place. We had a real sense of anticipation as it came time to publicly pass out the awards for James's 11–12 year old division.

As the speaker called out the third place winner, the other boys at the banquet table began to look to James, knowing that he would be recognized next.

With video camera in hand, Anne was positioned at the back of the banquet room, filming this scene for the family archives.

The head master said, "And finishing second this year..."

At this point, James was about to approach the podium to receive the reward he had earned.

Then the master of ceremonies did something unexpected. Instead of calling out James's name, he called out another boy's name. A kid whom James had beaten on a weekly basis.

Shock fell upon James's face. Anne kept videoing thinking that maybe we had all miscalculated and James had actually come in first place. But his name wasn't called out then either. As he slumped down in his seat, he realized that he had been passed over for some unknown reason.

Here was one dejected little boy when this awards presentation was over. James had earned second place through hard work and honest competition all summer. He had practiced day after day under the hot sweltering sun. When it was too sizzling hot for the other boys to play, James was out on the golf course working hard and improving his game. And he had consistently played well all summer, finishing in the top three almost every week.

So what went wrong? It seems that because he had played with the older boys for two weeks, he was rendered disqualified by the tour officials— something that even the tour officials later acknowledged was a questionable interpretation and something that they had failed to tell James when he came back down to his own age group.

I happen to believe that God allowed it for a purpose, and that purpose was to help teach our family a valuable life lesson. Life is not fair. This is not a perfect world in which we compete. Hard work is not always rewarded by men.

If our children work hard simply to be recognized by men, they will be very disappointed in this life because their performance will not always be properly appreciated or awarded. We must teach that ultimately they must strive and compete for God's reward. He alone judges righteously, rewards impartially, and compensates fairly.

Men, we must teach this kind of God-awareness to our children. As they grow in their God-consciousness, so will their estimation of the virtue, the character, and the reward of their work. If we can instill this, a legacy of responsibility will be passed on with great care to our children.

SENDING YOUNG WARRIORS INTO BATTLE

A Legacy of Strength

DO NOT PRAY FOR EASY LIVES. PRAY TO BE STRONGER MEN!
DO NOT PRAY FOR TASKS EQUAL TO YOUR POWERS.
PRAY FOR POWERS EQUAL TO YOUR TASKS.

—*Philip Brooks*

A few years ago for our youngest son John's birthday, Anne and I gave him a toy set of the full armor of God. Produced by a Christian manufacturer, each piece of the armor resembled Paul's passage on spiritual warfare in Ephesians 6.

You should have seen John's excitement as he ripped opened his birthday present. With a burst of energy, he began to put on each piece of the armor—the belt of truth, the breastplate of righteousness, the shoes of peace, the shield of faith, the helmet of salvation, and the sword of the Spirit. Right before my very eyes, my son was transformed into a young warrior ready for battle!

With visions of greatness in his mind, my normally reserved little boy was now ready to storm the gates of hell. His full battle dress gave him a new found confidence and a sense of invincibility.

For weeks, John was a terror in our household, jumping out from behind doors, ready to cut off his brothers from the land of the living. With his shield raised and his sword drawn, he would charge his sister, yelling like a martial arts fighter in a Grade B Kung Fu movie.

Quite frankly, we were all relieved when that plastic set of God's armor finally wore out and somehow "mysteriously" disappeared.

STORMING THE GATES OF HELL

In this chapter, we will see the armor that we must help our children put on as they face the daily battles of spiritual warfare all around them. Not one that is plastic and comes in a box. Nor one that deteriorates and crumbles under the weight of child's play. But one that is supernatural, impenetrable, and is put on by faith. I'm talking about fathers sending young warriors into battle against a formidable foe. A foe that requires the full armor of God.

If our children are to live victoriously in this world, we must leave them a legacy of strength—a strength that is supernatural and spiritual, a strength that is sovereignly supplied by our Commander-in-Chief. The only way our young kids can overcome Satan and escape his snares is for them to be equipped with God's invincible battle array—the full armor of God.

In this chapter, I want to look at what is the central passage in all of the Bible which deals with spiritual warfare—Ephesians 6:10–17. No section of Scripture more clearly reveals the invisible warfare being fought all around us than this passage. Here is an arsenal of truth with which every father must equip his children if they are to live victoriously over the enemy.

Men, I want you to look at this familiar passage with me in a new and fresh way. I want to put a new spin on these verses, not in its interpretation, but in its application. We will see this passage through the paradigm of fathering and reexamine our responsibilities toward our children. Admittedly, every time I've looked at these verses in the past, I've only considered how they related to me personally. But now, I want us to consider how these verses should impact our children.

The truth is, we are sending our children into a world filled with evil, and they must be outfitted in God's full battle array if they are to escape unharmed. The bullets are real out there. And it's only going to escalate. As the end of the age approaches, the Bible says the world will be growing worse and worse, not better and better. Consequently, their need for God's armor is not going away. The Bible tells us:

> But realize this, that in the last days difficult times will come. For
> men will be lovers of self, lovers of money, boastful, arrogant, dis-

obedient to parents, ungrateful, unholy, unloving, irreconcilable, malicious gossips, without self-control, brutal, haters of good, treacherous, reckless, conceited, lovers of pleasure rather than lovers of God. (2 Timothy 3:1–4)

With prophetic insight into the future, Scripture describes the terrible dangers of the last days which are rapidly approaching. This is precisely the world into which we are presently sending our children.

But the Spirit explicitly says that in later times some will fall away from the faith, paying attention to deceitful spirits and doctrines of demons, by means of the hypocrisy of liars seared in their own conscience as with a branding iron, men who forbid marriage and advocate abstaining from foods, which God has created to be gratefully shared in by those who believe and know the truth. (1 Timothy 4:1–3)

Concerning the last days, Jesus said these signs would intensify dramatically, like a woman in childbirth. When that moment occurs, the excruciating pain will come closer and closer together. Therefore, these latter times will become pregnant with iniquity as we await the return of Christ to deliver us from our troubles. It is such evil that awaits our children and demands our sober attention.

THE BATTLE IS HERE

Dads, are you aware of the evils confronting your children? They won't have to wait for college to face the lure of the world. They are facing unparalleled evil even now while they are living at home with you. Today, they are being bombarded on every side by sinful pressures and seductive temptations—many of which you and I never dreamed of facing as a child.

As the twenty-first century approaches, we have become like ancient Israel in those days immediately before their Babylonian captivity. The prophet Isaiah said they were a generation who had forgotten how to blush. Sin was so rampant that nothing shocked them anymore. They were so inundated with sin that they were desensitized to it.

Men, that's precisely the kind of society into which we are sending our children. We are a generation of "unblushables," and nothing shocks us anymore. We've seen it all!

As we send our children off to school, they are being faced with mounting pressures and temptations—even in many Christian schools. Listen, my children can not even pick up something as seemingly innocent as the sports page of our local paper without being hit between the eyes with ungodly temptation because of the sensual advertisements. And this says nothing of the magazines and mail order catalogues that enter our home.

If our children are to escape undefiled in the conflict, they must be clad in the full armor of God. We would be sadly naive to think that Satan is only targeting us dads. The wolf often preys upon the weakest lambs, those youngest ewes at the rear of the flock, because they are the easiest catch. So, it is imperative that our children are protected by the full armor of God.

Allow me now to introduce us to the verses that we will examine in this chapter. As we read them, think about how they apply to your children and how they must dramatically impact our fathering. Here's what the apostle Paul says:

> Finally, be strong in the Lord, and in the strength of His might. Put on the full armor of God, that you may be able to stand firm against the schemes of the devil. For our struggle is not against flesh and blood, but against the rulers, against the powers, against the world forces of this darkness, against the spiritual forces of wickedness in the heavenly places. Therefore, take up the full armor of God, that you may be able to resist in the evil day, and having done everything to stand firm. Stand firm therefore, HAVING GIRDED YOUR LOINS WITH TRUTH, AND HAVING PUT ON THE BREASTPLATE OF RIGHTEOUSNESS, and having shod your FEET WITH THE PREPARATION OF THE GOSPEL OF PEACE; in addition to all taking up the shield of faith with which you will be able to extinguish all the flaming missiles of the evil one. And take the HELMET OF SALVATION, and the sword of the Spirit, which is the word of God. (Ephesians 6:10–17)

In this section, the apostle compares the protection our children need with the armor of an ancient Roman soldier. As Paul pens these verses, he is imprisoned in Rome and probably chained to a soldier wearing just such armor. Consequently, he has the perfect object lesson immediately before his eyes—a captive audience, if you will. Here is what every father must instruct his children to put on if they are to escape unscathed in this world.

CHARGE #1:
DADS, RECOGNIZE THE WARFARE!

Put on the full armor of God, that you may be able to stand firm against the schemes of the devil. For our struggle is not against flesh and blood, but against the rulers, against the powers, against the world forces of this darkness, against the spiritual forces of wickedness in the heavenly places.

EPHESIANS 6:11–12

In these verses, several key words and phrases describe the reality of the spiritual warfare all around that confronts our children. The first word is "schemes" (verse 11). It is the Greek word *methodia* from which we get the English word "method" and carries the idea of cunning, craftiness, and deception. The term was used in the first century to describe a wild animal that would stalk its prey. That's how Satan is stealthily pursuing our children. "Your enemy, the devil, prowls about like a roaring lion seeking someone to devour" (1 Peter 5:8).

You know as well as I do, our kids are in a war—a fierce and terrible war for their souls. Our children are under attack and the devil would love nothing more than to steal our kids and take them captive into his kingdom.

Let's wake up! Satan has picked up the scent of our children and is hunting them down. The evil one is lurking in the thicket as they are walking to school, and hiding behind protective cover as they are playing in the backyard. He is ready to pounce upon and devour them.

Suppose you were driving in your car this afternoon and you heard over the radio that there had been a tragic accident at the local zoo—a lion had just escaped. Then you heard a police update and the ferocious lion was last sighted just a couple blocks from your house. And suppose that you had just talked to your wife on the phone moments before, and you knew that she was there along with your precious children, playing together in the backyard.

I'll guarantee you one thing, you'd head immediately to a phone to call and warn your wife. You would act quickly to protect her and your children. No dad would be so foolish as to just shrug it off and head to lunch—not if a lion was loose.

FIGHT LIKE A MAN

Mark it down, there is a lion prowling around your house, a lion far more serious, far more deadly, than those at the zoo. I'm talking about the serpent of old, the devil. We must warn our family and be certain that they're safe and protected.

Men, spiritual warfare is not child's play. Satan is not simply seeking to injure our children—he's seeking to devour them.

In addition, Paul says that "our struggle is not against flesh and blood" (verse 12). The harm that threatens our children is an invisible warfare fought against the unseen powers of darkness. What follows is a brief description of the evil empire that opposes our families. Paul classifies four divisions in Satan's administration—"the rulers, the powers, the world forces of this darkness, the spiritual wickedness in the heavenly places." Here is Satan's ranking of demons describing the various levels in his hierarchy. One thing is sure, there is a high order of demons that is very organized and highly sophisticated.

You see, the devil is a master strategist who has laid plans to harm your family. And his covert activity is *very well* conceived. There is intricate design and precise purpose to Satan's plans to ambush your family. He is extremely well set up, systematized, and strategized in his schemes to kidnap your children.

Dads, this spiritual warfare is all around our children. We ourselves must first see the invisible enemy that is surrounding them if we are to warn them. As we try to navigate our children through the uncharted waters of this world, we must understand where the last lion sighting was reported. Where was Satan last seen stalking our children?

First, *in the schools*. Humanistic thinking controls many of our schools and is indoctrinating our children at an early age. A man-centered world view, situational ethics, evolution, rewritten history, political correctness, sexual promiscuity, and alternative lifestyles—all these are man's deviations from God's Word and are a part of the core curriculum that is being taught in many classrooms today. Men, we must warn our children because they are in the devil's cross hairs.

Second, *in the media*. Much television is relentless in its attempts to recruit our children for the enemy's camp. Some sitcoms portray woefully dysfunctional marital relationships, rebellious children, homosexual bit players, immorality, foul language, coarse jesting, and sexual innuendoes. Mini-series have become primetime pornography. MTV, HBO, and the like are pumping Satan's filth into our dens and living rooms like a backed-up sewer. Even many seemingly innocent cartoons have a blatant agenda of sorcery and New Age thought. Are you aware of this?

Third, *in their toys*. Have you walked through a toy store lately? You ought to. It would be quite an education. An occult atmosphere hangs over many toy departments where a "dungeons and dragons" motif is prevalent, complete with sorcerers, witches, wizards, and grotesque characters from the underworld. Many video and computer games are blatant in their demonic allusions.

Fourth, *in their music*. Ever spiraling downward, the music industry has fallen to new lows in the message that they promote to our young people, to say nothing of the perverted lifestyles of those who sing and play on the albums. No father can afford to be ignorant of the powerful influence that music can hold over their children. Listen to much of the rap music lately? It is filled with vile lyrics which are sexually explicit, cop-killing, women debasing, and God-taunting.

Dads, are you aware of the music that your children are listening to? Have you taken the time to listen to the words of the songs that our children hear? I think that some of you would be shocked to hear what's being sung and what your children are listening to. This will require some major monitoring on your part to sensor out that which is even remotely inappropriate for your young ones to hear.

Fifth, *in the movies*. Films today are explicit in their graphic portrayal of evil, sex, and violence. Adultery, immorality, the occult, foul language, and violence all color most of today's movies in heavy doses. Even many of the new animated films have sinister characters which are planting lies in the minds of our children. We can't afford to be naive or ignorant and allow our children to head off to just any movie.

Fathers, do you have family standards for the movies that your children can watch? Do you oversee what your children are viewing? Are you willing to be considered prudish if you say no to certain movies?

All these battlefields—school, the media, toys, music, and movies—are where Satan is aggressively trying to win over our children. But we are of the light and we must see with discernment. Our spiritual antenna must constantly be up and ever be on red alert.

CHARGE #2:
DADS, ALERT YOUR CHILDREN!

Finally, be strong in the Lord, and in the strength
of His might... Therefore, take up the full armor of God,
that you may be able to resist in the evil day,
and having done everything, to stand firm.
EPHESIANS 6:10,13

The fact is, these are not days in which our children can be undecided, neutral, or halfhearted in the face of such growing evil all around them. We are so surrounded by sin these days, I fear that our kids are losing their resolve to stand fast and resist it. Rather than resisting Satan, many young people are giving in to his enticements. But we must rally our children to hold firm in their convictions. If they are to escape this warfare unharmed, they must firmly hold their ground. Compromise, even to the slightest sin, will spell defeat.

Victory necessitates that they "be strong in the Lord" (verse 10). Overcoming Satan's advances can be accomplished only in God's supernatural power. "Stand firm" (verse 11) is a military term which pictures a soldier holding a critical position while under attack. It pictures an army under attack, refusing to go into retreat, refusing to back up, choosing to hold its ground. That's exactly how our children must stand firm against Satan.

With deepening resolve, our children must choose to "struggle" (verse 12) against the demonic hordes of Satan's kingdom. This word "struggle" pictures hand-to-hand combat which was the way ancient warriors fought in the days of the New Testament. Because they didn't have long-range Scud missiles and other sophisticated weaponry, war was fought one on one, jaw to jaw, face to face, hand to hand. This pictures the close struggle in which our children will find themselves.

In addition, "struggle" also refers to the wrestling matches of the day in ancient Rome. Gladiator battles were life and death struggles, fought before thousands of spectators who flocked together to witness this barbaric sport. In these deadly battles, the victor would walk away alive and his opponent would be left dead on the floor of the coliseum. In the arena, it was either kill or be killed.

That's exactly the way spiritual warfare is. Our children must understand, especially as they grow older and advance into their teenage years, that there is no neutral ground. No peace treaty can be signed with Satan. There can be no conscientious objectors to this war. No spiritual pacifists can sit this one out. To the extent that they are able, our children must understand the hand-to-hand combat with Satan in which they find themselves and choose to "resist in the evil day" (verse 13).

"The evil day" is that time when Satan most aggressively advances his attack. We must understand there is an ebb and a flow to spiritual warfare. There are times when Satan realizes it is opportune to launch a surprise attack, and times when it's not (Luke 4:13). Satan is a brilliant strategist who will seek to gain the upper hand when our guard is down.

Men, it will be that way in our families. This means we must keep alert and be dressed in readiness if we are to resist in the evil day.

CHARGE #3:
DADS, EQUIP YOUR CHILDREN!

Put on the full armor of God, that you may be able
to stand firm against the schemes of the devil.
For our struggle is not against flesh and blood,
but against the rulers, against the powers, against
the world forces of this darkness, against
the spiritual forces of wickedness in the heavenly places.
EPHESIANS 6:11–12

There must be a conscious effort on our part to equip our children with the full armor of God. To every Christian—and this includes our children—Paul says, "Put on the full armor of God" (verse 11). Again, he says, "Take up the full armor of God" (verse 13). The repetition serves to underscore that our kids must always have on the full armor of God—all six pieces. Two of the six pieces of armor is not good enough. Putting on five out of the six pieces is not good enough.

Can you imagine, for example, the Dallas Cowboys lining up to play the Pittsburgh Steelers in the Super Bowl, and when the Cowboy offensive line runs out onto the field, they are fully equipped in their uniform except one piece—their helmets? That would be ludicrous! No way could they win. It would be pointless for them to even bother playing the game if the Cowboys didn't have on their helmets. Each piece is vitally important.

Or can you imagine the Cowboys playing the Super Bowl in their bare feet? It wouldn't matter how good they are, or how committed they are. If they didn't have on their cleats, they couldn't win.

In exactly the same way, each piece of God's armor is strategic and absolutely critical for victory. Let's consider the significance of each piece of the armor and how it relates to our children. Here's how our kids must dress every day.

1. PUT ON THE BELT OF TRUTH

The first piece of God's armor which Paul describes involves the belt of truth. He begins by saying, "having girded your loins with truth" (verse 14). In ancient times, a Roman soldier wore a tunic, a long flowing robe which covered his body. It had holes cut out through which the soldier would place his head and arms and it served to keep out the weather's elements. When it came time for battle, a soldier would gather up his long robe and tuck it into his belt so that he would not trip as he advanced into battle. But if a soldier didn't pick up his robe and tuck it into his belt, he wasn't ready to fight.

This imagery paints a picture that communicates readiness for spiritual warfare. There are two ways Bible teachers interpret girding oneself with the "belt of truth." It can either refer to a knowledge of doctrinal truth, or to an attitude of truthfulness, meaning a genuine commitment and readiness to fight. Personally, I believe it is the latter.

It seems that Paul's reference here is to an attitude of truthfulness in which our children are genuinely committed to Christ. This calls for whole-hearted readiness to stand for Christ and resist the devil. Our children can ill-afford to be lackadaisical, as it relates to the sinful allurements confronting them. They must be fully surrendered to Christ and genuinely committed to Him, because if not, they're going to take one step into battle and fall flat on their faces.

So, the first thing our children must do is be fully devoted to Christ. They need to tuck in their tunic and be prepared for battle with the enemy. Our job is to help them grow in their commitment to the Lordship of Christ. Admittedly, this will be a process that grows over time, just as it is in our lives. But small acts of obedience now will lead to greater responses of obedience later. Ultimately, they must each make their own decision to purposefully follow Christ in every area of their lives.

Bottom line, until this decision is made, there can be little victory over the advances of Satan.

2. PUT ON THE BREASTPLATE OF RIGHTEOUSNESS

In ancient times, a soldier's breastplate was absolutely essential when going into battle. This strategic piece of the armor covered his entire torso protecting the heart, lungs, intestines, and other vital organs from enemy attack. It was usually made of leather onto which overlapping pieces of metal, or animal hooves or horns were sewn.

In the day of battle, this is exactly the protection our children need. "The breastplate of righteousness" means to live in daily, moment by moment obedience to God. It is a life lived in conformity to the Word of God. This piece of the armor is a holy life lived according to the standard of God's Word and in the power God provides.

Why is this so important? Because when our children allow sin to go unchecked in their lives, it allows Satan the opportunity to gain a foothold (Ephesians 4:27). Like an invading army establishing a beachhead on foreign soil, so Satan seeks every opportunity to establish a stronghold in our hearts. When we sin, he desires to dig a foxhole and become entrenched in our lives, leading to greater satanic access in the future. But living a clean and pure life slams closed the door to our hearts and keeps Satan out.

Men, our kids must have a commitment to Christ that is real and genuine. They must live in daily obedience to the Lordship of Jesus Christ if they are to resist temptation and stand strong against Satan. An uncommitted life is an unguarded fortress.

A couple of summers ago, I preached through the passage about the temptation of Christ in the wilderness. One of the points for application that I made was to encourage the congregation to memorize particular verses of Scripture which would combat specific areas of temptation. As we sought to put this into practice at home, we had our children think through areas of personal struggle in their lives, and then we helped them find verses that rebutted each of those temptations.

Next, they memorized a corresponding verse that would lead to victory over each particular struggle. Over the next weeks and months, as they were tempted to fall into old patterns of sin, we encouraged them to call to mind that particular verse and to choose to obey it. I can honestly say that we saw progress in each of their lives as they chose to stand firm on God's Word.

Listen, that's precisely what putting on the breastplate of righteousness is all about. It is encouraging our children to choose to live consistently in obedience to God's Word.

3. PUT ON THE SHOES OF PEACE

The third piece of the armor listed by Paul is shoes. A Roman soldier wore these into battle, enabling him to stand. They usually had pieces of metal or nails attached to the bottom like spikes or cleats. This was to give him greater traction as he fought. His very life depended upon it.

Spiritual footwear is equally important in warfare for our children. They must put on the shoes of peace if they are to stand against sin. Our children must know that they are saved and are at peace with God. They must know with assurance they have taken their stand with Christ and they are on God's side of this conflict.

This is not a reference to evangelism because God has never called us to convert the devil. Such a thing is impossible. This passage refers to our spiritual warfare against Satan and his demons. Our children need to know on whose side they are on. They need the assurance of their salvation.

I'll never forget the last Sunday evening service I preached at my previous church before coming to Dauphin Way, not because of what occurred during the service, but for what happened at the end. After preaching a powerful sermon on the rich young ruler, I had the joy of leading two people to Christ.

During the time that I was explaining the gospel to these people, my son James, then eleven years old, kept saying, "Dad...Dad..." But before he could finish what he was trying to say to me, I cut him off, "James, you'll just have to keep it until later."

I figured that he was trying to tell me something about our plans after church. That would just have to wait until I took care of leading these people to Christ. But James kept intruding which, quite honestly, was starting to annoy me.

After both these people had trusted Christ with me, I was walking out of the sanctuary on a spiritual high. What a meaningful way to conclude fourteen years of ministry. Then I felt a tug on my sleeve. It was James.

Somewhat less irritated this time by James's persistence, I said, "Now tell me James, what couldn't wait?"

With tears streaming down his cheeks, he said, "Dad, I don't know if I'm saved."

Well, you could have knocked me over with a feather. I had been so preoccupied with leading others to Christ that I had neglected my own son's inquiry. Because James had prayed with me years earlier, it never dawned on me that he was under conviction himself.

We went back into my office and had a time of prayer. I believe that James had already been saved, but needed to be sure. This was a time to drive a stake down and make certain he belonged to Christ.

In actuality, James was putting on the shoes of peace and establishing the assurance of his salvation. This was absolutely necessary before he could do battle against Satan. He needed to know where he stood with God before he could stand against the devil.

Dads, do you know if your children have on the shoes of peace? Do they have the assurance of their salvation? Do they know without question that they belong to God?

4. PUT ON THE SHIELD OF FAITH

Just as we have an order to the way we get dressed, so had a Roman soldier as he was getting dressed for battle. Having put on the belt, the breastplate, and the shoes, now it's time to take up the shield. So, Paul writes, "Taking up the shield of faith with which you will be able to extinguish the flaming missiles of the evil one" (verse 16).

Now, there were two shields which Roman soldiers used in New Testament times. The first type was a small shield about 2 feet by 2 feet that was strapped to a soldier's forearm. It was used in very close combat. The other shield was larger, approximately 2 1/2 feet by 4 feet, and was large enough for a man to hide behind and protect his entire body.

In battle, waves of soldier's would march forward, side by side, forming a moving wall against the enemy. As the opposing army would shoot flaming arrows, these large shields would be held up for protection. It is this second shield—the larger of the two—that is spoken of here.[1]

The shield of faith provides protection from Satan's incoming missiles. This shield is a basic trust in God for daily provision and help. It is looking to God to meet your every need, whether it be physical, emotional, spiritual, relational, or financial.

What are these flaming missiles of the evil one? Ancient soldiers would dip their arrows in pitch, set it aflame, and shoot it at the enemy, hoping that it would stick and engulf the warrior in fire. In self-defense, the soldiers would coat their shield to try and make it fireproof. But if one of these flaming missiles struck you, you would go up in smoke.

These flaming missiles picture Satan's fiery temptation aimed at our hearts. I believe that it represents a specific temptation—the temptation to distrust God. If you are tempted to distrust God, then you are lured to trust someone else—such as a teacher, scout leader, boyfriend, girlfriend, or coach. We must know that God is sufficient for everything, but Satan will be constantly attempting to cause us to doubt or deny this.

We have seen this applied in our son's life just within the last year. As you have probably picked up by now, we are pretty involved in sports at our house. Last year this particular child had a struggling year in both basketball and golf. Having a twin brother with whom he competes day in and day out doesn't help! But, through much prayer with him, and our encouragement to trust God, we have seen a genuine maturity in the midst of disappointment. We have seen him go from responding with frustration and, at times, very bad attitudes, to a quiet dependence on God. This was definitely a time for our son to hold up the shield of faith to extinguish the fiery missiles of discouragement.

Dads, your words are a powerful motivation that will encourage your children to trust God. Like Aaron who helped hold up Moses' arms as he lifted high the staff in battle, so we must help our sons and daughters hold high the shield of faith in their battles.

Dads, we must teach our children to put their trust in Him, no matter what. They must know how to put their trust in God in every circumstance, trial, or test in which they find themselves. No lesson will ever be more important to learn.

Solomon instructed his son, "Trust in the Lord with all your heart, and lean not on your own understanding. In all your ways acknowledge Him, and He will make your paths straight" (Proverbs 3:5–6).

5. PUT ON THE HELMET OF SALVATION

Next, Paul says that our children must put on "the helmet of salvation." This is not talking about being converted to Christ. That has already occurred, or the one putting on the armor wouldn't be fighting Satan.

The word salvation means deliverance. Moses stood before the Red Sea, lifted his staff and said, "Stand back and see the salvation of the Lord" (Exodus 14:13). By faith in God, the sea parted and God's people were delivered. God will make a way where there is no way. That's what the word salvation really means—a deliverance from trials and troubles.

Salvation comes in three aspects—past, present, and future—or justification, sanctification, and glorification. It is assumed at this point that our children have already converted to Christ. That's justification, or immediate salvation from the penalty of sin. This salvation refers both to sanctification which is the progressive, daily salvation from the power of sin, and glorification, which is the ultimate, future salvation from the presence of sin.

This helmet of salvation is the hope we have that God is able to deliver us through every temptation and out of every trial, and that one day He will deliver us into his very presence. We have great hope that God will always come through for us. He will never fail us. He will never disappoint us.

Ancient soldiers wore a heavy helmet to deflect the blow of a broadsword swung at one's head. The sword mentioned in the later half of this verse was a small dagger. But the other sword that was used was a large broadsword about four feet long. The enemy grabbed it by both hands and swung it through the air indiscriminately, trying to chop off a man's head. This helmet served to ward off such a blow.

This broadsword pictures the attempts of Satan to discourage us. When he is allowed to strike us without any defense, we lose hope and grow weary. But wearing the helmet of salvation, we can always defend ourselves from Satan's advances. Hope allows us to combat discouragement and believe that God will come through for us.

We all wrestle with discouragement—even our children. But the helmet of salvation overcomes those moments of despair.

6. PUT ON THE SWORD OF THE SPIRIT

Finally, our children must take up "the sword of the Spirit which is the Word of God" (verse 17). What is this sword?

This sword was a small dagger carried on the belt of a Roman soldier. It was used in hand-to-hand combat to be thrust into the side of the enemy. Because the dagger was small, it could be used with precision—as opposed to the large broadsword that would be swung wildly through the air. This sword was used with deadly accuracy—representing the precision with which we are to use the Word of God to overcome a specific temptation.

Our children cannot have just a broad general knowledge of some vague truths about the Bible. They must have a precise knowledge of the Word before they can use it with accuracy. When Jesus was tempted in the wilderness, He quoted a specific passage of Scripture to overcome a particular temptation. This is how we must teach our children to use the Word of God.

As a result, we must immerse our family in the Scriptures. They must know specific truths from specific verses in the Word of God. When they are confronted with choices, their lives must be governed by the Word which the Holy Spirit will bring to their minds for use against Satan.

The Spirit of God pulls out of our heart and puts into our hand specific scriptures to answer particular temptations. We must help our children establish a building reservoir of truth from which the Holy Spirit can give recall.

David taught, "How can a young man keep his way pure? By keeping it according to Thy word...Thy word I have treasured in my heart, that I might not sin against Thee" (Psalm 119:9, 11). As our children are surrounded by a sea of impurity, they are faced with temptation to lead impure lives. How can they stay pure? Not on their own, that's for sure. Only through the power of God's Word, as they study it with the mind, store it in the heart, and obey it with the will.

When they are in the heat of battle and are suddenly hit with a temptation, the Spirit of God must convict their heart with the Word of God and lead them to victory. This is what we want for our kids—why? Because we are sending them out into battle. We can't dispatch them to the front lines in their pajamas. They must have on the full armor of God.

Men, we must know that there's a spiritual warfare going on out there. We must help our children take a stand against Satan, sin, and temptation. And we must equip them with a full set of armor:

- *Belt of truth:* genuine commitment to Christ
- *Breastplate of righteousness:* daily obedience to Christ
- *Shoes of peace:* assurance of salvation in Christ
- *Shield of faith:* complete trust in Christ
- *Helmet of salvation:* confident hope in Christ
- *Sword of the Spirit:* precise use of the Word of God

Just as we help our children when they are young to get dressed in the morning, we must help them now to put on the full armor of God. While this is a decision that they only can make, we bear the responsibility to make sure they are fully equipped. Why? Because we never know when Satan will attack.

THE WARFARE ALL AROUND US

Not long ago, I took our family to lunch after church on Sunday. We had just experienced God's power in a wonderful worship service at Dauphin Way. As we were seated in a very reputable restaurant, I had no idea what awaited us.

Once seated, I noticed two long tables of middle-aged women next to us. Suddenly, a band began to play what resembled a pagan fertility dance. It sent the room rocking. Boy, did the natives get restless! Before we knew it, these women with champagne glasses and cigarettes in hand began to sing at the top of their lungs and parade around the tables in "soul train" fashion. Little did I know that this was a warm-up for Mardi Gras.

I immediately got up to ask for another table. And while I was gone, this band of renegades descended upon our table. As they circled our table, these drunk women lassoed our children's necks with strings of beads, beckoning them to join in. It's a good thing I was on the other side of the room or I would have purged the temple of the money changers.

There sat our precious little children having no idea what in the world was going on. Their eyes were bugging out of their heads as they witnessed the enticement of the devil. As fast as I could, I gathered my flock and saturated that place with our absence.

Men, as you maneuver your family through this world they, too, will be confronted with unexpected lures and enticing entrapments strategically placed by Satan.

You never know how Satan and his demonic forces will encircle your family to wage war against you. Therefore, we must make certain that our "troops" always have on the full armor of God and stand ready to resist the evil one.

Why?

We're sending young warriors into battle.

PART 3

BEQUEATHING
A LEGACY

CHAPTER 13

YOU STAND TALLEST
ON YOUR KNEES

The Legacy Secured by Prayer

EVERY TIME WE PRAY, OUR HORIZON IS ALTERED, OUR ATTITUDE TO THINGS
IS ALTERED, NOT SOMETIMES BUT EVERY TIME, AND
THE AMAZING THING IS THAT WE DON'T PRAY MORE.
—*Oswald Chambers*

A spiritual legacy can only be passed down in God's strength, not our own. And that requires prayer.

George McCluskey understood this.

As a young husband, McCluskey made the commitment to invest one hour a day in prayer for his future family not yet born. He prayed that his children would come to know Christ personally and would follow Him closely. Eventually, George expanded his prayers to include his future grandchildren and great grandchildren.

In an amazing way, God answered those prayers.

George had two daughters who committed their lives to Christ and each married men who went into full-time ministry. Between them, the two couples had four girls and one boy. Each of the four girls married a minister, and the boy became a pastor.

But the power of George McCluskey's prayers didn't stop there.

The first two grandchildren born to the next generation were boys. And upon graduation from high school, the two cousins chose the same college and became roommates. During their sophomore year, one of the boys decided to go into the ministry. The other didn't. Understandably, he felt some pressure because he chose not to continue the family legacy. Instead he chose to pursue psychology.

This young man earned his doctorate and eventually wrote books to help parents raise their children which became best sellers. Although he didn't enter the pastorate, he has ministered to millions through a radio program heard on more than a thousand stations each day. Today, his influence upon the family is felt around the world.[1] His name?

James Dobson.

Incredibly, George McCluskey's prayers have been answered many times over. Not only are they still influencing his family four generations removed, but families around the globe as well. On his knees, his family legacy was prepared, passed on, and preserved. He stood tallest on his knees.

WANTED: PRAYER WARRIORS

Men, we must do the same. Our family legacy will endure only through prayer. Throughout the course of this book, we have talked about the legacy that we must leave our children—a legacy of core values and godly virtues. As the spiritual leaders of our homes, we want Jesus Christ to be real in the lives of our children. This is the only legacy worth leaving. And it can only be passed down through prayer.

Once our children have put on the full armor of God—as we discussed in the last chapter—the battle isn't over. It's only just begun. Victory in the lives of our children is won on our knees in prayer. As fathers, we must intercede on their behalf with the God of heaven who alone can cause them to stand strong in this world. Consequently, the apostle Paul writes:

> With all prayer and petition pray at all times in the Spirit, and with this in view, be on the alert with all perseverance and petition for all the saints. (Ephesians 6:18)

Men, we want our children to be all that God desires them to be. If we will lift up our hands on the mountain top, they may prevail victoriously in the valley. It is only as we lift up our prayers to the Lord that the legacy will become theirs.

In this chapter, I want us to learn *how* to pray for our children. If they are to be successful in life, we must know how to pray effectively for them. As intercessors, we must pray for them:

- *Comprehensively*—"with all prayer and petition"
- *Consistently*—"pray at all times"
- *Confidently*—"in the Spirit"
- *Carefully*—"be on the alert"
- *Constantly*—"with all perseverance"

Billy Graham says there are three keys for having a successful evangelistic Crusade—prayer, prayer, and prayer. The same is true for effective fathering. We could also say there are three keys for successfully passing down the legacy to our children—prayer, prayer, and prayer. Look with me now and consider how we can pray effectively for our children.

CHALLENGE #1:
DADS, PRAY COMPREHENSIVELY!
With all prayer and petition.
EPHESIANS 6:18A

A father's prayers for his children should be all-encompassing in their extent.

In other words, our intercession should include a rich variety or diversity. That's the idea behind Paul's words "all prayer and petition" (verse 18). What's the difference between prayer and petition? And how does the one build upon the other?

"All prayer" means *all kinds,* or *all types,* of prayer. The word "prayer" is generic and includes the many different expressions of prayer. "Petition" refers to specific requests, or individual supplications. From these words, we learn that all kinds of prayers should be offered to God on behalf of our children, not just petitions. There should be a diversification about our prayers for our children.

You may be thinking "What different kinds of prayers should I, as a dad, be offering on behalf of my children?" To answer that question, I think it would be helpful for us to hear again the words of Jesus Christ who gave us specific teaching on this subject. This is the breadth that Christ said we should have in prayer:

And He said to them, "When you pray, say: Father, hallowed be Thy name. Thy kingdom come. Give us each day our daily bread. And forgive us our sins, for we ourselves also forgive everyone who is indebted to us. And lead us not into temptation." (Luke 11:2–4)

These verses are commonly referred to as our Lord's model prayer. They were never intended to be words memorized and rotely repeated back to God verbatim. That breeds vain repetition. Rather, they were given to serve as a skeleton outline to guide us in the various aspects of our prayers. According to our Lord's instruction, there are five basic categories of prayer: *adoration, submission, supplication, confession, and protection.* I want us to briefly examine each aspect and consider how they should relate to our prayers on behalf of our own children.

First, *adoration.* Jesus said that we should begin our prayers, "Father, hallowed be Thy name" (verse 2). That means praising God for who He is and for what He has done, especially for our family. To "hallow" His name means to exalt His name, to reverence His character, to magnify His greatness. Nothing is more important in prayer than to glorify God, even prayer offered for our children.

Accordingly, every father should begin his prayers for his family with praise. As the family priest who goes to God on behalf of his children, our prayers should commence with an earnest plea that God's name be glorified in and through their lives. Herein is the highest design and ultimate purpose of every family—that God be glorified. We should pray, "Father, we exist as a family to honor and glorify You. God, work in and through the lives of our children to lift high Your name on the earth so that You will be glorified."

Along this line, let me add one more essential aspect of our praise— thanksgiving. As fathers, we should be constantly offering thanks to God for what He has done in the lives of our children. The Bible says, "Enter His gates with thanksgiving, and His courts with praise" (Psalms 100:4). This verse says, thanksgiving and praise go hand in hand together.

Thank Him for the many successes your children have enjoyed. *Thank Him* for the positive influences in their lives. *Thank Him* for the personal growth and spiritual development that you see in them. *Thank Him* for the dangers from which they have been shielded, or delivered. *Thank Him* for the many victories God has won in their lives.

Men, let us cultivate a thankful heart of praise to God for our children.

Second, *submission*. After we praise God's greatness, we should then humble ourselves and seek His will on behalf of our children. Jesus said we are to pray, "Thy kingdom come" (verse 2). This aspect of prayer petitions God's rule and reign to be made real, specifically in this case, in the lives of our family.

The purpose of prayer is not to get *our will* "rubber-stamped" in heaven, but for *God's will* to be accomplished on the earth. Regarding our family, we should ask God that His sovereign pleasure be done in our home. Prayer is not dictating to God what we want, but asking Him what He wants and then humbly submitting to it.

That's how Jesus prayed. In the Garden of Gethsemane, under the shadow of the cross, He said, "Father, not My will, but Thine be done" (Luke 22:42). And that's how we should pray for our children, "God, not my will, but Thy will be done." Men, we must pray, "God, what is *Your* will for my child? Show us *Your* will. Where do *You* want my daughter to go to school? Where do *You* want us to live? What activities do *You* want my son to participate in?" Let us be careful not to impose our agenda upon our children and then attach God's name to it, but earnestly seek God's will. As I prayed about coming to pastor the church I now serve, a significant part of my prayers related to the lives of my children. I found myself praying, "God, how will this move impact my children? God, what is your will for the lives of my children? Is this where you want them to grow up?"

Third, *petition*. Next, Jesus instructed us to pray, "Give us each day our daily bread." Only after we have submitted to God's plan (verse 2) can we ask for His provision (verse 3). We must know His will before we can know what to request. His "daily bread" refers to the various needs that we have as a family, whether they be physical, emotional, or spiritual needs. Both big and small things, we should bring to God in prayer.

A woman once asked the great preacher, G. Campbell Morgan, "Can I ask God for little things in my life, or only big things?" Morgan replied, "My dear lady, can you think of anything in your life that is big to God?" Certainly not! *Everything* in our life is small compared to God.

So, ask God to meet your family's needs. Nothing is too big for Him to handle, nothing too small for Him to care.

As we intercede for our children, we should be specific in our requests. In the parable that immediately follows the Lord's model prayer, we read:

And He said to them, "Suppose one of you shall have a friend, and shall go to him at midnight, and say to him, 'Friend, lend me three loaves; for a friend of mine has come to me from a journey, and I have nothing to set before him.'" (Luke 11:5–6)

This man is specific in his requests, "I need three loaves of bread." He prayed for a specific—*bread,* a specific kind of bread—*loaves,* a specific number of loaves—*three.* This is how precise God wants us to be on behalf of our children. To the extent that we perceive God's will, we should pray, "God, would You help my child with *such and such* a character issue?" Or, "Would You provide *such and such* an amount of money for their school tuition?" Or, "Would You open the door to get *such and such* a job?" Bottom line, be specific.

Fourth, *confession.* Furthermore, Jesus taught us to pray, "And forgive us our sins, for we ourselves also forgive everyone who is indebted to us" (verse 4). As dads, we ourselves need to confess our sins to God, seeking His forgiveness for our many failures. When we name our sin to God, He cleanses and restores us, making us the dads we need to be.

There is a condition for receiving God's forgiveness. Only to the extent that we forgive others will God forgive us. Jesus also said, An unforgiving heart forfeits God's forgiveness. But the heart that freely forgives others will freely receive forgiveness from God (Matthew 6:14–15). Let us never nurse a grudge, especially with our wife or children, or God will not forgive us.

There will be times when we need to forgive our children, just as there will be occasions when we need to ask for their forgiveness. When we do, we must seek their forgiveness. Such confession leads to answered prayer. The Bible says, "Confess your sins to one another…The effective prayer of a righteous man can accomplish much" (James 5:16–17).

I'm ashamed to admit it, but I lost my cool with one of my boys when they were young. As I was correcting him, he failed to pay attention to me which only upset me more. Unfortunately, I spoke to him with sarcasm that wounded his tender heart. As I saw tears well up in his eyes, the Holy Spirit convicted me deeply. I knew I needed to ask for his forgiveness. With tears of my own, I went over and hugged him and said, "Son, would you please forgive me. I was absolutely wrong to say what I just said."

He said, "Dad, I forgive you."

Men, I needed that. If I had not confessed my sin, my guilt would have remained and my prayers would have had no power. If we want to be powerful in prayer, especially for our children, we must maintain a pure heart with our children. We must continually confess our sins if we are to be a spiritual leader at home.

Fifth, *protection.* Jesus, finally, taught us to pray, "And lead us not into temptation" (verse 4). As this relates to our family, we must ask the Lord to deliver our children from the subtle power of the evil one. We ought to be pleading with God for His protective hedge to be around our children, requesting that He deliver them from weak moments in which they are vulnerable to sin. Like us, they have chinks in their armor in which they are exposed and susceptible to Satan's advances. We must intercede for our family and ask God to guard them from such temptations.

This is what praying comprehensively for our children encompasses. It means that we pray with "all prayer and petition" as Paul says, which includes *adoration, submission, supplication, confession,* and *protection.*

Do your prayers for your family have this kind of breadth? In which of these areas are you strong? In which are you weak? What steps could you take today?

CHALLENGE #2:
DADS, PRAY CONTINUALLY!
Pray at all times.
EPHESIANS 6:18B

Paul goes on to say that we must *always* be in prayer for our children. When the apostle says, "pray at all times," this includes a father's prayers for his children.

To "pray at all times" does not mean that we are to pray out loud verbally every moment of every day, with our heads bowed, eyes closed, and knees bent. If we did that, there would be no time to do the other things that God calls us to do—things like work, witness, Bible study, fellowship, worship, and service to God. So, what does this mean?

Praying continually means living with an attitude of prayer, being always dependent upon God in prayer, being ever ready to bring whatever crosses our path to God in prayer. As soon as we face a need, that's when we are to pray. In other words, we should live with a continual God-consciousness. It means always bringing the needs of our children to Him in prayer.

As the spiritual leader of our home, when something good happens to our children, we should stop immediately and thank God. When we see them in need or trouble, we should seek His help immediately on their behalf. When we discover them entrapped with wrong actions or selfish attitudes, we should promptly pray for God's conviction to come to their lives. Or, as they are away from home, we should continually pray for their protection from temptation. The point is, in whatever circumstance our children find themselves, we are to be standing with them in prayer—*continually!*

Take yesterday for example. After teaching an early men's Bible study, I drove to my children's school where my daughter Grace Anne appeared in a school play. As I was en route, I prayed in the car that God would help her remember her lines, project her voice, and not be too shy.

Let me tell you, she was outstanding! Normally shy and reserved in front of people, I was astounded that she did so well. In fact, I squinted my eyes to make sure that it was really her. As I sat in my seat, I offered a silent prayer, "Lord, thank you for what a great job she did. God, show me how else she could use that ability in the future for You."

Later that day, God brought to my mind my twin boys who were in the midst of exam week. So, I asked Him to help them study and score well because I knew they were struggling with a few courses in school. I'm grateful to tell you, one of my sons who was not doing particularly well that semester made the highest grade in the class. Now, that's an answer to prayer! I tell you that, not as a doting dad, but as a grateful father, knowing that God answers prayer. When I heard the report, I breathed a sigh of relief and said, "Thank you, Lord."

And when I got home at the end of the day, I was confronted with several decisions that I had to make regarding my boys. Consciously and deliberately, I said silently, "God, I need your wisdom in this matter. Tell me, what do we do here?" And He did.

That's what it means to be continually in prayer for our children. Do you pray at all times for your kids? If not, why not pick up the pace.

CHALLENGE #3:
DADS, PRAY CONFIDENTLY!
Pray…in the Spirit.
EPHESIANS 6:18B

We can believe that God hears our prayers and will answer them to the extent that they are in accordance with His will. When Paul says, "pray in the Spirit," he is referring to Spirit-empowered, Spirit-directed prayers for our children. This is praying in concert with the Spirit. Such prayer for our kids will be in alignment with the mind and the will of the Spirit.

The other alternative to praying "in the Spirit" is praying in the flesh. And praying in the flesh is pushing our own selfish agenda ahead of God's. Either we are praying God's will in the Spirit, or we are praying our own will in the flesh. I can assure you this, God will only answer prayers that are in the Spirit.

The apostle John wrote, "And this is the confidence that we have before Him, that if we ask anything according to His will, He hears us. And if we know that He hears us in whatever we ask, we know that we have the requests which we have asked from Him" (1 John 5:14–15). Now, that's praying with confidence!

Adrian Rogers says, "The prayer that starts in heaven gets to heaven, we simply close the circuit." In other words, Spirit-directed praying discerns the will of God and then prays it back to God. Prayer is not overcoming God's reluctance, but finding His readiness to do His will.

All this translates into having great confidence in our prayers for our children. As we pray in the Spirit, we have boldness to approach God's throne and ask whatever we need knowing that we will desire that which the Spirit desires.

That reminds me, a little boy was saying his bedtime prayers late one night with his dad. "Lord, bless Mommy. Bless Daddy." He prayed and then shouted, "And God, GIVE ME A NEW BICYCLE!"

The dad said, "God's not deaf, son. You don't have to shout when you ask for a new bicycle."

"Yeah, I know," he said, "but Grandmom is in the room next door and *she is* deaf."

Listen, if it's God's will, we may ask boldly and expect to see Him work powerfully in their lives. God promises to answer our prayers according to His will. Again in Luke 11, Jesus instructed us:

> Now suppose one of you fathers is asked by his son for a fish; he will not give him a snake instead of a fish, will he? Or if he is asked for an egg, he will not give him a scorpion, will he? If you then, being evil, know how to give good gifts to your children, how much more shall your heavenly Father give the Holy Spirit to those who ask Him? (Luke 11:11–13)

Arguing from the lesser to the greater, Jesus said, if we as earthly fathers with sinful natures know how to give good gifts to our children, how much more will our heavenly Father, who is holy and free from all evil, delight to give them good gifts. Certainly, it is inconceivable that we would give a poisonous snake or a dreadful scorpion to our kids. To an infinitely greater extent, it is *absolutely impossible* for God to give our children anything except the very best.

Now, here's the point. When we as earthly fathers come before God, our heavenly Father, something happens. Prayer changes things. We could call it "Father Power." Something special happens when earthly fathers come before their heavenly Father in prayer for their earthly children, especially when they are spiritual children.

Even now, my own father continues to pray for me. And when he does, I am certain that the power of God is released in my life. I am convinced that, from an eternal perspective, I am serving God as I am today because of my father's prayers. Even when I have wavered, he has prayed confidently for God to guide me and place me where I am and use me. Although in his seventies, my dad is still having an impact on my life through his prayers.

Men, let us do the same for our own children. Let us pray boldly, confidently, and courageously that God will bless them greatly. As we pray "in the Spirit," their lives will be dramatically affected.

CHALLENGE #4:
DADS, PRAY CAREFULLY!
And with this in view, be on the alert.
EPHESIANS 6:18D

As we pray for our children, every father must do so with our eyes wide open. Paul continues, "be on the alert" (verse 18). This means we are to be always watching out for our children, ever bringing to God their personal needs and pressing struggles. Alertness pictures the way a guard keeps his watch, always looking out for the enemy. Every dad must be manning his post in prayer.

The apostle Peter adds, "Be of sound judgment and sober spirit for the purpose of prayer" (1 Peter 4:7). In other words, we pray, not as in a fog, but with clarity of vision, always watching out for the enemy.

Our children are being constantly confronted with all kinds of evils, pressures, and temptations. Spiritual warfare demands that we be in prayer for them with all alertness. We discussed in the last chapter some of the devices of the evil one that are confronting our children on a daily basis. You may want to reference back and recall some of those. Consequently, we need to pray with an understanding of the sinful world in which our children live. We must carefully pray that our alertness and their defenses will be always up. Gentlemen, this is serious stuff.

I heard a speaker in a conference ask, "Do you believe God answers prayers?" Of course, my answer was, "Yes, I do."

But then he hit us right between the eyes with his punch line, "You only believe it as much as you practice it." Ouch! If we truly understand the seriousness of the spiritual warfare which our children face, then our prayers for them will greatly increase.

Men, be on the alert in prayer!

CHALLENGE #5:
DADS, PRAY CONSTANTLY!
Pray...with all perseverance.
EPHESIANS 6:18E

I don't know about you, but I give up too easily in prayer. If I don't see immediate results, oftentimes I quit and fail to carry through with it any further. I bet you can relate to this. By nature, we are an impatient and impetuous lot.

That's why Paul concludes this verse by saying, "pray with all perseverance" (verse 18). This does not say, *some* perseverance. Nor *much* perseverance. But *all* perseverance. In other words, we are to stay after it in prayer, never letting up. All too often, we assume God's delays are God's denials. We think our requests must not be God's will if we pray once and it is not immediately answered by sundown. If God's answer is not according to our time schedules, then we want to give up and move on to something else. But to the contrary, we are to *keep on* seeking, *keep on* knocking, *keep on* asking on behalf of our children (Matthew 7:7–11).

Maybe you heard about the woman who accidentally left her expensive diamond broach, an irreplaceable family heirloom, in a hotel restroom? When she got home, she discovered that her broach was missing and immediately called the hotel. She told the manager of her desperate situation and he immediately went to look for it.

After searching for a few minutes—what seemed to be an eternity to the frantic woman—he found her broach, put it in the hotel safe, and returned to the phone to tell her the good news.

But to his amazement, when he picked up the phone, she had hung up! In her impatience, she did not wait long enough for the positive answer which was on the way.

Truth is, gentlemen, we are all like this when we pray. We aren't willing to persevere on our knees and wait on God. Honestly, I'm sure it would amaze and astound us to know how often God is on the way with the answer to our prayers, but we grow impatient and hang up too soon, failing to receive what God has for us.

Listen to what Jesus said in the following parable. He couldn't make it any more clear. The point is—don't give up in prayer!

And He said to them, "Suppose one of you shall have a friend, and shall go to him at midnight, and say to him, 'Friend, lend me three loaves; for a friend of mine has come to me from a journey, and I have nothing to set before him'; and from inside he shall answer and say, 'Do not bother me; the door has already been shut and my children and I are in bed; I cannot get up and give you anything.' I tell you, even though he will not get up and give him anything because he is his friend, yet because of his persistence he will get up and give him as much as he needs." (Luke 11:5–8)

Don't miss this! This is not teaching that God is reluctant to help our children when we pray. Nor that we can wear God down in prayer and coerce Him to do what He really doesn't want to do. What Jesus is saying is our persistence in prayer will prevail because God delights to do His will through His people as they pray with persistence.

You've probably heard about one lanky shortstop who was considered too tall to play in the big leagues. Yet he kept plugging away and finally made his way onto the roster of the Baltimore Orioles. On May, 1982, this gangly 6'4" infielder played the first game of what was to become known as "The Streak." Over the next fourteen years, he never missed a game!

In a day when few "superstars" play hurt, and in a game requiring incredible endurance, this man played with a regularity never before seen. Some 2,131 games later, he set the all-time record for consecutive games played by a major leaguer, breaking the once thought unbeatable mark held by Lou Gehrig.

His name is Cal Ripkin.

We see from his career that greatness comes not solely from our ability, but also from our availability. As it was with this future Hall of Famer, so it is with dads in prayer. Our greatness as fathers comes as we constantly persevere in prayer, day in, day out, interceding for the needs of our children.

Men, what kind of a streak do you have going in prayer? Are you in the game on behalf of your children? Or, do you need to get off the bench?

No matter what the score may be, you can get into the starting lineup and start a streak of your own. Don't ever forget, the legacy you leave for your children is won through your prayers. Step up to the plate, men, and go to bat for your kids.

You stand tallest on your knees.

CHAPTER 14

WHAT DO YOU WANT ON YOUR TOMBSTONE?

The Legacy That Endures

A GOOD CHARACTER IS THE BEST TOMBSTONE...
SO CARVE YOUR NAME ON HEARTS AND NOT ON MARBLE.
—*C.H. Spurgeon*

For the one who leaves a legacy, death never means the end. It's only the beginning.

Years ago, Winston Churchill, Great Britain's former prime minister, planned his own funeral before he died. He did so believing that the end of his life marked, in actuality, the beginning of a bright and glorious future.

Churchill died on January 24, 1965 and the nation mourned. His funeral was held at Saint Paul's Cathedral in downtown London, where just two decades earlier Nazi planes had dropped their bombs and threatened the very existence of England. But now, through Churchill's dramatic leadership, the world was safe and this historic church became the collecting place for the world's greatest leaders as they came to pay their respect for Britain's last Lion.

Kings and queens, princes and prime ministers, presidents and high-ranking dignitaries from more than 110 nations were in attendance, including President Dwight D. Eisenhower, French President Charles de Gaulle, Chief Justice Earl Warren, Queen Elizabeth II and the Duke of Edinburgh. All of England watched via the BBC broadcast.

Those present reflected upon the greatness of this courageous man. Having led England through the darkest hours of her long and storied history, his words were loaded with vision and faith as he inspired the English people to rise up and resist the Nazi tyranny. The indomitable will of this man inspired all of England to victory in her "finest hour."

But now, Britain's former prime minister was dead.

At the end of the funeral, per Churchill's request, a bugler was positioned high overhead in the vaulted dome of Saint Paul's Cathedral. Immediately after the benediction was pronounced, a lonely trumpeter pealed the heart-rending notes of "Taps"—the universal signal that says the day is over.

But, in reality, all was *not* over.

Not for Churchill, nor for England.

Another bugler was positioned high above on the other side of the massive dome. But this second trumpeter played another set of notes, very different than the first, answering with "Reveille"—the universal signal that a new day has dawned.[2]

When you leave a legacy, all is not over.

That was the message Churchill wanted trumpeted at his funeral. The end of his life was only the beginning of a glorious tomorrow for his beloved country. His legacy would live on. The end notes of his life did not signal "Taps," but "Reveille."

Although he was gone, the British people possessed freedom and a great hope with which to face the future. His life had been bequeathed as a legacy of resolve and strength to his countrymen. Now Churchill is gone. But his life remains.

They called it a funeral. But it was in truth, a triumph.

That's precisely the way each of us can bring our days to a fitting end. Not with such pomp and celebration as Churchill, but with equal confidence that a fitting legacy has been passed on from us to the next generation. Death need not signal the end of our life, but only a new beginning. Because when we pass down a spiritual legacy to our children, our influence continues long after we are gone.

For the father who dies without leaving a legacy of core values to his loved ones, his funeral signals "Taps"—his day is *over*. But the dad who leaves behind a spiritual legacy of godly virtues, the conclusion of his life signals "Reveille"—his life *continues*.

I began this book by asking you to look ahead and consider your own funeral. Just as Churchill planned his funeral before his death, so you and I must plan ahead and consider how we want our lives to end. We must do so now *before* we die.

By that, I do not mean we must plan the order of service at our funeral. Rather, we must determine today what we want to be the lasting influence upon our children. We must ask ourselves, what legacy do you want your family to take with them after you pass off the scene? What will be the lasting inheritance that you pass down to them long after you are gone?

Unless Christ comes first, the day of our death will surely come. In light of our imminent departure, we must plan now what values we want chiseled into the hearts of our children by the intentional influence of our lives.

What legacy we desire to leave will determine the choices we make today. Secondary issues pale in significance in the light of eternity. And what really matters becomes primary as we anticipate that day.

When you come to the end of your life, what must you hear your children say for you to feel that your fathering was successful? What would you want them to say that would cause you to think that your life as their father had been well spent?

As men of faith, our consuming passion must be to leave behind a spiritual legacy. Specifically, we must pass down an inheritance of core values that are rooted and grounded in Jesus Christ. We must bequeath an inheritance of godly virtues that money can't buy and death can't take away.

BACK TO THE FUTURE

I was reminded of this a few years ago after speaking for a Billy Graham Crusade in New Jersey. With a few extra hours before catching my return flight home, I was asked what I would like to do before departure. As a child, I had grown up just a few miles away and had never had an opportunity to be back in almost forty years. So I asked if I could be driven to my old hometown of Dover, New Jersey.

As we drove into town, it was really strange. I had no map nor any directions. And yet, I knew exactly where I was and where I was going. I was flooded with memories of my early childhood, a time that was instrumental in the establishment of my faith. My instincts led us directly to my old house where I had lived as a young boy.

Over forty years later, it was all just like I remembered it.

I walked up to the front door and knocked. A woman answered, and after introducing myself, I shared my story with her. She invited me in, and I immediately saw the stairs leading up to my old bedroom. It was terribly important for me that I see that room again, because it was there that I had prayed to receive Christ as a young boy.

At first, she refused because the house was a mess. But my persistence overruled and she finally allowed me to go up. I walked up the stairs and, as I entered my old bedroom, I was overcome with emotions.

In my mind's eye, I could still see it just the way it had been four decades earlier. I could see my father sitting on my bed reading Bible stories to me every night. I could see the vivid pictures of Christ in that Bible story book. I could hear him praying with me as he tucked me in bed. It was there in that room that I had prayed and given my life to Christ. My faith was rooted and grounded in the soil of his faith.

Tears ran down my cheeks as I reflected upon those nighttime sessions with my father. I thank God for a dad who led me to faith in Christ. Like a successful relay race, the faith had been passed on to me and I grasped it and began to run with it.

Isn't that the way it ought to be? Every dad's faith should be reproduced in the lives of his sons and daughters. Every dad should leave a legacy of faith with his own children that will be theirs for time and eternity.

That is what we live for.

That is what we must die for.

CHAPTER 1

1. Howard G. Hendricks, Christian Home 726: Unpublished class notes, Dallas Theological Seminary, Dallas, TX, 1979.

2. Pete Maravich and Darrel Campbell, *Heir to a Dream* (Nashville, TN: Thomas Nelson Publishers, 1987), p.225.

CHAPTER 2

1. Swenson, Richard A., *Margin* (Colorado Springs, CO: Navpress, 1992), p.152.

2. *U.S. News and World Report,* January 1989.

3. Swenson, *Margin,* p.152.

4. Kenneth Langley, "To Illustrate...Choices," *Leadership,* Spring (1989): p.44.

5. Frank F. Furstenburg Jr. and Andrew J. Cherlin, *Divided Families: What Happens to Children When Parents Part* (Cambridge, MA: Harvard University Press, 1991), p.11.

6. "Intervarsity Staff Workers Respond to the Crisis," *InterVarsity,* Spring (1989): p.14.

7. Mueller, *Understanding Today's Youth,* p.41.

8. National Association of State Boards of Education, *Code Blue: Uniting for Healthier Youth* (Alexandria, VA: 1990).

9. Robert Byrd, "Most High School Kids Aren't Virgins, Survey Finds," *Johnstown (PA) Tribune Democrat,* 4 January 1992.

10. Josh McDowell and Dick Day, *Why Wait? What You Need to Know about the Teen Sexuality Crisis* (San Bernardino, CA: Here's Life Publishers, 1987), p.23.

11. Joseph P. Shapiro, "The Teen Pregnancy Boom," *U.S. News and World Report,* 13 July 1992, p.38.

12. "Teenage Pregnancy," *Search Institute Source,* November 1985, p.1.

13. Dinah Richard, *Has Sex Education Failed Our Teenagers?* (Pomona, CA: Focus on the Family Publishing, 1990), p.24.

14. NASBE, *Code Blue,* p.3.

15. Lloyd D. Johnston, Patrick M. O'Malley and Jerald G. Bachman, *Drug Use Among American High School Seniors, College Students and Young Adults 1975-1990,* vol. I (Rockville, MD.: National Institute on Drug Abuse, 1991), p.9.

16. Charles Colson and Nancy R. Pearcy, *A Dance with Deception* (Dallas, TX: Word Publishing, 1993), p.178.

CHAPTER 3

1. Richard Hoffer, "Mickey Mantle: The Legacy of the Last Great Player on the Last Great Team," *Sports Illustrated,* August 1995, pp.27–28.

2. Richard Jerome, "Courage at the End of the Road," *People Weekly,* August 1995, pp.77–82.

CHAPTER 4

1. James S. Hewett, ed. *Illustrations Unlimited* (Wheaton, IL: Tyndale House Publishers, Inc., 1988), p.332.

CHAPTER 5

1. *Classic Cases: The Estates of Famous People* (Chicago, IL: Dearborn Financial Publishing, 1990), p.1.

2. James P. Lenfestey, "Catch of a Life Time," *Reader's Digest,* February 1989, pp.111–12. Reprinted with permission from the February 1989 *Reader's Digest.*

CHAPTER 7

1. Steve Farrar, *Finishing Strong* (Sisters, OR: Multnomah Books, 1995), p.36.

2. Chuck Swindoll, *The Strong Family* (Portland, OR: Multnomah, 1991), pp.101–102.

Chapter 9

1. Swindoll, *The Strong Family,* p. 84.

2. Gary Ezzo and Anne Marie Ezzo, *Growing Kids God's Way* (Chatsworth, CA: Micah 8:8, 1993), pp.209–210.

3. Percy Livingstone Parker, ed., *The Journal of John Wesley* (Chicago, IL: Moody Press, n.d.), pp.105–106.

4. Gary Ezzo, *How to Raise Your Family* (Sun Valley, CA: Grace Community Church, 1985), p.35.

Chapter 10

1. Adrian P. Rogers, *God's Way to Health Wealth and Wisdom* (Nashville, TN:, Broadman Press, 1987), p.12.

2. Warren W. Wiersbe, *The Bible Exposition Commentary* (Wheaton, IL: Victor Books, 1989), p.55.

3. John MacArthur Jr., *The MacArthur New Testament Commentary: Ephesians* (Chicago, IL: Moody Press, 1986), p.319.

4. Wiersbe, *The Bible Exposition Commentary,* p.55.

Chapter 11

1. Edward K. Rowell, ed., *Quotes and Idea Starters for Preaching and Teaching* (Grand Rapids, MI: Baker Books, 1996), p.98.

Chapter 12

1. MacArthur, *Ephesians,* p.357.

Chapter 13

1. Steve Farrar, *Point Man* (Portland, OR: Multnomah, 1990), pp.154-55.

2. Carolyn Bennet Patterson, "The Final Tribute," *National Geographic,* August 1965, pp.199–225.